A note from the a

I have written this book ha
Independent Money Manager ʀor over three
decades.

Firstly, who are the sharks? Well, it's better
than it used to be. The large banks and
insurance companies with direct sales forces
are powerful and dominate, but they are the
sharks. They offer expensive contracts and
hidden fees.

This book will guide you through the maze,
help you to save money, teach you how to
invest, and show you how to choose an
adviser who works for you, not the sharks and
who is not a puppet controlled by a company.

"You will get the best advice if you pay for the advice, rather than if the sharks pay for the adviser."

Chapters

Chapter 1
Round peg, square hole

In my early days, when I first became a financial adviser in 1989, I started knocking on doors for a large British insurance company.

I sold a regular savings plan for £100 per month. That was a big deal back then. When I went to the office to hand in the application forms, I expected a big "well done young man", as back then it was the largest policy I had sold - almost get out the brass band and dancing girls.

However, I was taken to one side by the manager and asked if I could go back to the client, come up with a story of why they would be better to do 10 separate policies at £10 each rather than one for £100 per month.

I thought this was wrong. 10 times the application forms. 10 times the work for what? Then the penny dropped. I was not cut out to be a direct sales adviser tied to one company.

See, this is the dirty little secret... charges make the investment world go around.

With a £100 policy there was a monthly policy fee of £2.00 per month - 2%. With a £10.00 policy there was a £2.00 policy fee, but times that by 10 and that's £20.00 per month to be collected in fees - 20% of the premium. A BIG win for the big, bad insurance company, but not so hot for my client.

If you then add on the 5.5% bid-offer spread (initial charge) and then the annual management charge (AMC) 1.5% pa resulted in a 27% charge.

What a rip off by the company. That's when I fell out with the company and left on principle, and that started my journey as an independent fee-only adviser.

I was never going to fit as an adviser selling only the company's products.

Now a generation later, it's not really changed. The sales reps (or they may call themselves consultants, advisers, and one company even call their commission-only salespeople partners) that work for the banks, building societies and large insurance companies sit the same side of the desk as the company they represent, not your side of the desk to represent you, hold your hand and guide you through the maze.

Beware of the salesman

See, your future is important, but my role is to guide you through the minefield, help you to buy investments products at a fair price and create diversified portfolios that meet your needs and not the investment company's needs.

Chapter 2
No to a big cheque

Why do some advisers work for large Insurance companies, selling overpriced products that deliver underperformance and a lack of diversification?

Did they sell out? Selling your soul to the devil, is a well-known expression.

These advisers simply put their needs first and ahead of the client needs, in my opinion.

Back in 1996 I was 30, I was an independent adviser, with a small group of clients that trusted me, liked me and respected me.

Then a very large investment company came to see me and offered me all sorts to give up my independence, to join them and sell only their products.

In short, I was offered £990,000 as a transfer fee or a golden hello to join them, plus shares and many other benefits.

I was 30, married with two young kids, a mortgage and little in savings. Was this a dream or a nightmare? I considered the future, but I said no, thank you. I walked away from the money, and that took courage, but I knew that I was not selling out and selling sub-standard products to my clients.

I believe everyone deserves the best. Why would anyone settle for below average knowingly? We all want the best for our family and our futures, so don't buy products from the travelling salesman whose office is the car seat.

Although I chose to say no, there were many advisers that did not. They sold out and took the money. Only they know how it feels, but the client is who we serve and not to be recommended second or third best.

I have always said, "Take the money off the table, what would the answer be?"

I took the money off the table in the decision. Money can seduce you. So, when faced with decisions, take the money off the table. See if the adviser is focused on themselves to sell the product that pays the most commission. Well, that's what you're going to end up with. Good for them. But maybe not right for you.

Some companies will pay a commission to their advisers for selling a product.

As an example, an ISA pays the adviser 3% and an Investment Bond pays 6% of the premium. The likelihood is you may end up with a bond, as the interest of the salesperson was put before yours.

So, staying and resisting golden handshakes, has allowed me to remain a fully Independent Wealth Manager, with my remuneration paid by fees from my clients only.

More importantly a good Independent Adviser, who works for you and represents you.

Chapter 3
Puppets on a string

Let me tell you a story about the difference between an independent adviser and that of a salesperson from an insurance company.

Back in 2009, I was fortunate to win Investment Adviser of the Year - voted via Money Facts.

During the global financial crisis, commercial property funds run into all sorts of difficulties, losing on average 40% of their value - at this stage, this is not relevant.

Under my coaching group, Dream Team Coaching, I ran a study group with some of the brightest and successful advisers. We met every 90 days to discuss industry issues. On the agenda this time were the threats to property funds.

I had a tool I used called TOSA - Threats, Opportunities, Solutions, Actions. We discussed the threats to property funds and the actions were to switch from property to another asset class, which was cash, as we felt there could be an impending crash in the commercial market from our data that we had gathered.

The decision was made to switch at no additional cost for our clients. We communicated with the clients as to why we had come up with these recommendations and what steps they needed to follow. We were successful in switching about 95% of our clients out of the sector before the funds became suspended and then the continued fall within the market. We had successfully switched over £50 million!

A few months later, at our next coaching day, I asked how everyone had got on with exercise and shared how we actioned the switches, our results and what the next steps were, as we continued to communicate with our clients.

Then I asked the guys who worked for the tied companies, the banks and insurance companies what they had done. They confessed they wanted to make the switches as they believed it was the right advice for the client, but the companies they worked for had forbidden the switches. They stated there was no danger to the clients and were quick to remind them that they worked for the company, not the client.

This is the fundamental problem when companies sell only their own funds - their interests are put ahead of that of the client. The result was they were not allowed to switch, their clients lost money in the short term - approximately 40% of the value.

Imagine you had £100k before, but after it's now only £60k, all because the company stopped the right thing from happening. It took, on average, five years for the funds to come back, and five years of lost growth, simply because the company controlled the distribution channels.

These advisers were literally puppets controlled by the evil empire of the insurance companies who put their own selfish needs ahead of their clients.

As an independent adviser, I could make my own informed decisions and action them. This showed I was right to be an independent and not a puppet controlled by the company's needs.

I was fortunate enough to have won a prestigious award, whilst some of my friends were dragged through social media and sued for not taking action. The companies hung the puppets out to dry. Their businesses were damaged and client relationships and trust lost.

So, the moral of the story is do not buy products from salespeople who only sell their own products. It's for a fat commission, and the host company will always control the investments. It's tough out there. Instead, stack the cards in your favour and not in the hands of the product provider.

Chapter 4
Smoke and mirrors

Hidden fees and half truths

How can you sail off into the sunset if your boat has got a hole in it?

What if it's slowly but surely taking on so much water that it'll sink before it reaches its destination?

I hate to tell you this, but most people are in exactly this position. They don't realise they are doomed to disappointment because of the gradual – but ultimately devastating – impact of excessive fees on their financial well-being.

They have no idea this is even happening to them. They have no idea that they are victims of a financial industry that is surreptitiously but systematically overcharging them.

Some investors believe they pay no fees at all to have a pension. This is the equivalent of believing that a KFC has no calories.

Some have no idea how much they are actually paying. In other words, they're blindly trusting the financial industry to look out for their best interests.

Remember, this is the same industry that tried to get me to sell 10 £10.00 policies rather than one £100 one.

It's the very same industry that brought about the global financial crisis!

You know the age-old saying 'Ignorance is bliss'? Let me tell you; when it comes to finances ignorance is not bliss. Ignorance is a disaster for you and your family.

This chapter will shine a laser on the subject of fees, so you know exactly what's going on. The good news; once you know precisely what's happening, you can put a permanent life-changing stop to it.
Excessive fees can destroy your nest egg.

Let's assume the stock market gives a 7% return over 50 years. At that rate, because of the power of compounding each £ Pound / € Euro or $ Dollar goes up to 30%.

But the average fund charges you costs of 2% which drops your average annual return to 5%.

At that rate, you get 10 £€ or $. So, 10 versus 30

You put up 100% of the capital, you took 100% of the risk, and you got 33% of the return.

Let me explain…

You forfeited two-thirds of your nest egg to line the pockets of money managers who took no risk, put in none of the capital, and often delivered mediocre performance!

Who do you think will end up with the ski lodge in Vail?

THE WOLVES OF WALL STREET

So, how do you pick the right funds? There are certainly enough to choose from. There are about 6000 unit trusts in the UK so it's safe to say the unit trust fund market is a tad saturated.

Why do so many companies want to be in this business? Because it's easy money.

The majority of financial professionals are intelligent, hardworking and thoughtful. But Wall Street has evolved into an ecosystem that exists first and foremost to make itself. It's made up of corporations whose purpose is to maximise profits for their shareholders. That's their job!

Since demonstrations in the late 90's, shareholders have become the tail that wags the dog, helping towards the global crash due to greed.

Even the best-intentioned employees are working within the confines of this system. They're under intense pressure to grow profits and are rewarded for doing so. If you – the client – happen to do well too, that's great! But don't kid yourself. You're not the priority.

The company or adviser puts you at the back of the pile, but it's your hard-earned tax paid money, your children's inheritance that they are taking. It turns out that the professionals aren't really any better at predicting the future than the rest of us.

To make matters worse, all this trading gets expensive. Every time a fund trades in or out of a stock, a firm charges commission to execute the transaction.

It's a bit like gambling at a casino: the house gets paid no matter what.

It gets worse! If your stock goes up, you'll also have to pay taxes on your profits when you sell the stock.

For investors in an actively managed fund, this combination of hefty transactions and taxes is a silent killer, quietly eating away at the fund's return. To add value after taxes and fees, the fund manager has to win by a really big margin. And, as you'll soon see, that isn't easy.

The Government again take no risk, put in no capital, but tax all of the gains. Remember, Dick Turpin stole from the rich to give to the poor. The Government steals from all of us.

This isn't the sexiest topic. But it should be! Because the largest expense in your life is taxes and paying more than you need to pay is insane. Especially when it's absolutely avoidable! If you're not careful, taxes can have a catastrophic impact on your returns.

Why should you care? Because your profits could be slashed by 30% or more unless you're holding the fund inside a tax-deferred account such as an ISA or Pension Fund. Fund Companies don't like to dwell on these tax issues, preferring to tout their pre-tax returns.

Imagine that over time you're losing two-thirds of your potential nest egg to fees – and you're giving up another 30% in unnecessary taxes. How much will really be left for your family's future?

Example

Here's another way to put this into perspective: an actively managed fund that charges you 3% a year is 60 times more expensive than an index fund that charges you 0.05%!

Imagine going to the pub with a friend. She orders a small white wine and pays £4.15, but you decide to pay 60 times more. Your price is a whopping £249! I'm guessing you'd think twice.

In case you think I'm being too extreme, let's consider the example of two neighbours, Alan and Rick. Both are 35 years old, and each has saved £100,000, which they decide to invest.

Over the next 30 years, the universe smiles on them, and each of them achieves a gross return of 8% a year.

Alan does it by investing in a portfolio of index funds that cost him 0.5% a year in fees. Rick does it by owning actively managed funds that cost him 2% a year.

By the age of 65, Alan has seen his nest egg grow from £100,000 to approximately £865,000.

As for Rick, his £100,000 has grown to only £548,000. They both achieved the same rate of return, but they paid different fees.

The outcome, Alan has 58% more money – an additional £317,000 for retirement.

Let's look at it if you pay monthly, and the benefit of compound interest.

Let's illustrate the impact of compounding:

Two sisters Helen and Charlotte decide to invest £300 a month. Helen gets started at age 19 and keeps it going for eight years and then stops adding to her pot at age 27 due to having children. In all, she saved a total of £28,800. Helen's money then compounds at a rate of 10% each year. By the time she retires at 65, how much does she have? The answer is £1,863,287. From that modest investment of £28,800, acorns into chestnuts.

Her sister Charlotte got off to a slower start. She partied and did not start to save until age 27. Still, she's a disciplined girl, and keeps investing every month until she's 65 – a period of 39 years. Her money also compounds at 10% a year. When she retires at 65, she's sitting on a nest egg of £1,589,733.

Let's think about this for a moment.

Charlotte invested a total of £140,000, almost five times more than the £28,800 Helen invested. Yet Helen has ended up with an extra £273,554. That's right; Helen ends up richer than Charlotte despite the fact she never invested a pound after the age of 27.

Can this be correct you ask?

By starting earlier, the compound interest she earns on her investments adds more value to her account than she could ever add on her own.

Let's imagine for a moment that Helen didn't stop investing at age 27. Instead, like Charlotte, kept adding £300 a month until she was 65. The result: she ends up with the nest egg of £3,453,020!

In other words, she has £1.86 million more than Charlotte because she started investing 8 years earlier.

That's the awesome power of compounding. Over time this force can turn a modest sum of money into a massive fortune.

Chapter 5
When a fee is really smoke and mirrors

When you make a decision on investing, you will take the time to compare the annual management fee, which the investment company will charge you for managing the fund, this is fair enough as there is nothing for nothing. But and this is a big but, are there any other fees not disclosed or swept under the carpet?

You need to know the TER (Total Expense Rate). This is the AMC (Annual Management Charge) and all other hidden fees added together.

On the following pages, you'll find some tables which highlight some interesting figures around hidden fees.

This table shows a selection of well-known companies with the advertised AMC, we can easily see what they are and could decide if it was based only on one area.

Asset	AMC %
Investec Diversified Income I Acc	0.79
Neptune Emerging Markets C Acc GBP	1.28
Baring Eastern Trust I Inc	1.03
JPM Asia Acc	0.93
JPM Europe Smaller Companies C Inc	0.93
Premier Ethical C Acc	0.92
Schroder European Opportunities Z Inc	0.93
Fidelity UK Opportunities W Acc	0.95
Threadneedle UK Absolute Alpha Z Acc GPB	0.88
Baillie Gifford Emerging Markets Bond B Inc	0.75

In this table, we have added the additional fees that were not disclosed. You can see that the additional fees have doubled the AMC. Outrageous charges with no transparency.

Asset	AMC %	Additional Expenses %
Investec Diversified Income I Acc	0.79	2.14
Neptune Emerging Markets C Acc GBP	1.28	1.37
Baring Eastern Trust I Inc	1.03	1.60
JPM Asia Acc	0.93	1.68
JPM Europe Smaller Companies C Inc	0.93	1.45
Premier Ethical C Acc	0.92	1.44
Schroder European Opportunities Z Inc	0.93	1.41
Fidelity UK Opportunities W Acc	0.95	1.09
Threadneedle UK Absolute Alpha Z Acc GPB	0.88	1.09
Baillie Gifford Emerging Markets Bond B Inc	0.75	1.14

You may think that is it, but in the next table, we prove otherwise. You will see the actual final answer. This is the AMC and the TER added together.

Asset	AMC %	Additional Expenses %	Total %
Investec Diversified Income I Acc	0.79	2.14	2.93
Neptune Emerging Markets C Acc GBP	1.28	1.37	2.65
Baring Eastern Trust I Inc	1.03	1.60	2.63
JPM Asia Acc	0.93	1.68	2.61
JPM Europe Smaller Companies C Inc	0.93	1.45	2.38
Premier Ethical C Acc	0.92	1.44	2.36
Schroder European Opportunities Z Inc	0.93	1.41	2.34
Fidelity UK Opportunities W Acc	0.95	1.09	2.04
Threadneedle UK Absolute Alpha Z Acc GPB	0.88	1.09	1.97
Baillie Gifford Emerging Markets Bond B Inc	0.75	1.14	1.89

WOW! A sub 1% AMC turns out to be 300% more expensive than advertised and disclosed. That is why total transparency is crucial, and therefore you need an adviser who works for you and is not working for and paid by the investment company.

Discretionary Fund Management (DFM)

DFM is another acronym for Discretionary Fund Manager. A DFM provides a service. They simply get on and invest your money and do as they see fit, within the risk levels that have been agreed.

However, there is a current trend that advisers who don't have the confidence or ability to advise on funds will pass the investment decisions to a DFM which results in an extra layer of fees.

The old saying 'too many pigs eating from the trough' springs to mind.

Many advisers will still charge an adviser fee of say 1% per annum and then pass you to the DFM who will charge their fee of say 0.5%.

That means you are now paying far more than you need to due to the greed of the advisers. Just think how many heads are in the trough feeding from your investments. These extra fees may not sound much, but it's your money, your kids' inheritance, your future income. All of these fees are eroding your wealth.

Let's have a look at the table below, showing again there is over 1% pa difference between the companies. This is just a short list as there are over 100 DFMs to choose from in the UK alone, but again it's your money and an extra layer of charges.

Fund	Total DFM Fee Based on a £250k
Rathbone Wealth	1.44%
Brewin Dolphin	1.20%
Close Brothers	1.20%
Quilter Cheviot	1.20%
Thesis	1.08%
Brooks Macdonald	0.90%
Investec	0.90%
Alpha	0.48%
Parmenion	0.36%
7IM	0.30%

My view is if you want a DFM go direct, don't go via an adviser, as this is an extra layer of unnecessary costs. If the advisers don't have the skill to do it themselves, maybe you should avoid that adviser.

Let's look at it in real money, say you have £500k and the investment grew at 6% PA compound for 10 years, if you saved 0.96% per annum on fees, this would save you an incredible £82, 906.78.

So, if you're going to use a DFM, make sure you're not double charged!

On the subject of DFMs, unfortunately now some companies known as consolidators, have bought in independent advisers so they can get the advisers to switch your money into their own DFM platforms.
There is a conflict of interest here, but it's fundamentally done to control the assets and add an extra layer of charges which are unnecessary and expensive to the client, as many clients are not aware of who owns who.

You should ask why the adviser does not have the skills, research abilities, and confidence to do it themselves but to continue to charge a full fee for now doing literally half a job.

DFMs do have a place, generally for funds above say £250k, but these advisers are placing small investments of below £10k into them, as the adviser's needs are put ahead of the client's.

You do have to question whose interests are put first. I think it's the advisers. In simple terms, if they are not up to the job, they should move over to let the good honest adviser lead the way, as they just muddy the water with their motives first which is wrong. The client should always come first.

Continuing with the subject of fees, we will show you where and how you can save money on fees.

Initial charges

The setting up of investments can vary hugely. Below is a table showing the difference in initial charges. They can also be referred to as Bids/Offers or set-up fees. Either way, it's a charge that is taken from your investment when you invest.

High Bid Offer Spreads (26th February 2018)

Fund	Sell Price	Buy Price	Spread
Marlborough Nano Cap Growth P Acc	158.14 p	174.05 p	9.16%
Schroder UK Real Estate	45.29 p	47.72 p	5.09%
Liontrust UK Micro Cap I Acc	140.47p	146.47 p	4.10%
Artemis UK Smaller Companies I Acc	1741.06 p	1800.94 p	3.32%
Schroder UK Smaller Companies I Acc	146.9 p	150.70 p	2.52%
Artemis UK Special Situations I Acc	618.62 p	629.63 p	1.75%
Artemis Capital I Acc	1683.37 p	1708.54 p	1.47%

With a 9.16% spread, that would be £9160 on a £100,000 investment, with other fees that could take up to 2 years to recover from!

High-Performance Fees

Henderson UK Absolute Return I Acc

Charges taken from the Fund under certain specific conditions	
Performance fee	20.00%*

*20% of any returns that, subject to a High Water Mark, the Fund achieves above the Bank of England Base Rate. The actual amount charged in the Fund's last financial year amounted to 0.74%.

For more information about charges, please see the "Charges" section of the Fund's prospectus.

City Financial Absolute Equity I Acc

Charges taken from the Fund under certain specific conditions
PERFORMANCE FEE: 20.00% of outperformance of 3-month GBP Libor with a high water mark

Black Rock UK Absolute Alpha

Charges taken from the Fund under certain conditions	
Performance Fee	20.00%#

20.00% of any returns that, subject to a high water mark, the Fund achieves above the LIBOR 3 Month Index. Further details are available in the Prospectus. The actual amount charged in the Fund's last financial year ending 31 May amounted to 1.51%.

Be aware of the hidden performance fee. This is a fee that should the fund perform well (hedge funds typically have one) there may be a 20% fee of the profits over say 15% to 20% per annum return. This is okay as you have made a healthy profit, however on the above examples they charged 20% of the profit against very low benchmarks. The Bank of England base rate is only 0.5% per annum.

Exit Charges

Other fees to look out for are exit charges. These are all being charged by the provider and are generally difficult to obtain information on.

Companies such as St James' Place Wealth Management, say they have no exit charges but have early withdrawal charges on some of their products such as pensions and investment bonds.

1 year - 6%
2 years - 5%
3 years - 4%
4 years - 3%
5 years - 2%
6 years - 1%

If you invest and need to withdraw early, you could end up paying £6000 in year one on a £100,000 investment.

A 6% charge for leaving the company is hard to justify, so be aware.

Switch Fees

A well-managed portfolio will be switched or rebalanced on a regular basis, but you need to make sure there are no switching fees. What you're really doing is selling a fund and buying a new fund, so it's vital that there are no hidden fees.

The table below shows switching charges for three companies.

Company	Switch Fees
Marlborough	Initial charge (typical initial fees for equity funds are 5%-5.25% - 4% discount to switch = 1%-1.25% switch charge
Invesco Perpetual	1% charge
Schroder	If going to single prices fund switch is free. If going to dual price again incur bid-offer spread and **charge around 1%**

Chapter 6
Market Risk

It's not sunny every day in paradise.

Do you remember how you felt in 2008 when the financial crisis savaged the global economy? Or maybe you're new to the market.

Do you remember the fear, the anxiety, the uncertainty that gripped us all when the world seemed to be falling apart?

The stock market and the property market collapsed. Big banks fell over like toy soldiers. Millions of good, hard-working people lost their jobs.

I was the Managing Director of a wealth management company at the time. We spent our time communicating and keeping our clients informed that the turbulence would pass.

Wouldn't it be wonderful if all that uncertainty had ended in 2008? Didn't you think the world would be back to normal by now? That the global economy would be back on track and grow dynamically again?

But the truth is, we're still living in a crazy world. All these years later, central bankers are still fighting an epic battle to revive economic growth.

You think I'm exaggerating? Well, think again. First world countries such as Switzerland, Sweden, Denmark, Germany and Japan now have 'negative' interest rates.
The whole purpose of the banking system is for you to make a profit by loaning money to banks so they can lend it out to others.

In this book I'm going to provide you with close to 30 years of experience, I'm going to bring you answers, share insights, so you can understand how to win even in these incredibly uncertain times.

Firstly, let's look at some insights…

This graph demonstrates the markets during 2000 - 2003

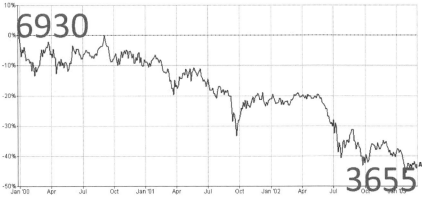

A - FTSE 100 TR in GB [-42.73%]

30/12/1999 - 28/02/2003 Data from FE 2018

This graph demonstrates the markets during 2007 to 2009

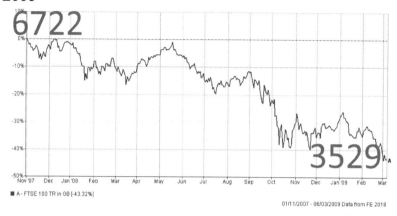

This graph demonstrates the markets 2009 to date

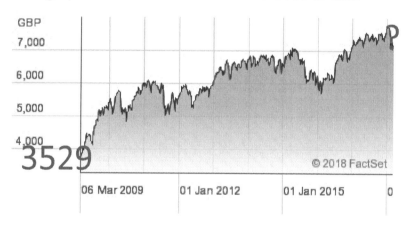

As we can see in the last two major drops, in excess of 40% was wiped off the values of people's investments if they were fully invested in the UK market.

If you were invested in a UK index-tracking fund, they might have been cheap, but there was no diversity. You would have walked off a cliff.

If this was a time when you were retiring, then the impact is very painful.

I wish it were that simple though. I can tell you this: most people find it really hard to sit tight and stay in the market when everything is going haywire.

Buy and hold tends to go out of the window. If you have nerves of steel that's great.

But if you want to know how the majority of people behave under stress, just check out a study by Dalbar, one of the financial industry's leading research firms.

Dalbar revealed the gigantic discrepancy between the markets returns and the returns that people actually achieve. For instance, the S&P 500 returned an average of 10.28% a year from 1985 – 2015, which means your money would double every seven years.

Thanks to the power of compounding, you'd have made a killing just by owning an index fund that tracked the S&P 500 over those 30 years. Let's say you'd invested £50,000 in 1985, how much would it have been worth by 2015?

The answer £941,613.61.

But while the market returned 10.28% per year, Dalbar found that the average investor only made 3.66% a year over three decades! At that rate, your money doubles only every 20 years. The result? Instead of a million, you end up with just £146,996.

What explains this massive performance gap?

In part, it's the disastrous effect of excessive management fees, outrageous brokerage commissions and other hidden costs. These expenses are a constant drain on your returns.

How can you help yourself?

Here's what you do have to do: you have to focus on what you can control, not on what you can't.

You can't control where the economy is headed and whether the stock markets will soar or plunge.

As I write this, the stock market has risen for eight years in a row, making this the second longest bull market. There's a widespread sense that we're due for a fall – what goes up must come down.

By the time you read this, the market may have already tumbled.

Nobody can accurately predict with any consistency where the financial markets are headed.

We all know that winter is coming and the stock market will fall apart, but none of us knows when winter is coming or how severe it will be. Does that mean we're powerless? Not at all.

When snow comes, do you want to be the one who's stuck outside, freezing in the bitter cold? Or do you want to be the one who's wrapped up warmly by the fire?

I want to show you how to avoid getting eaten by sharks.

One of the biggest obstacles to achieving financial success is the difficulty of figuring out who you can and cannot trust.

There are plenty of fantastic human beings working in the financial field – people who always remember their mother's birthday, who are kind to dogs and who have impeccable personal hygiene.

But they're not necessarily looking out for your best interests.

Most people who you think are providing unbiased financial 'advice' are actually bankers or are working for insurance companies who spend millions on marketing, even if they prefer to go by other titles.

They make hefty commissions by selling products or whatever else may pay for their next trip to the Bahamas.

This table is an example of how one company does it.

SJP Fund Name	Manager Name	SJP As %	Manager as %	Total charges as %
Alternative Asset Unit Trust Report	Black Rock Advisors	1.2	0.03	1.23
Gilts Unit Trust	Wellington Management International	0.83	0.1	0.93
Index Linked Gilts Unit Trust	BlackRock Investment Management UK	0.99	0.05	1.04
North America Unit Trust	Aristotle Capital Management	1.07	0.19	1.26

Actively managed fund companies charge huge fees in return for their services. Sounds fair enough, right?

The problem is, most funds do a terrific job of charging high fees but a terrible job of picking successful investments. One study showed that 96% of mutual funds failed to beat the market over a 15-year period! The result? You overpay for underperformance.

Even worse, those fees add up massively over time. If you overpay by 1% per year, it will cost you 10 years' worth of retirement income. This is what pays for annual sales trips, such as cruises and fancy hotels. It's your money!

Once we've shown you how to avoid funds that overcharge you could easily save yourself as much as 20 years of income.

If that's all you learn it will transform your future. I will also show you how to avoid salespeople who provide self-serving 'advice' that's hazardous to your financial health and how to find sophisticated advisers who aren't conflicted, not puppets on a string.

Chapter 7
Four Factor Focus

As the saying goes, 'when a person with experience meets a person with money, the person with experience ends up with the money, and the person with money ends up with experience.'

The Four Factor Focus is a very easy and straightforward way for all investors to focus on four core areas.

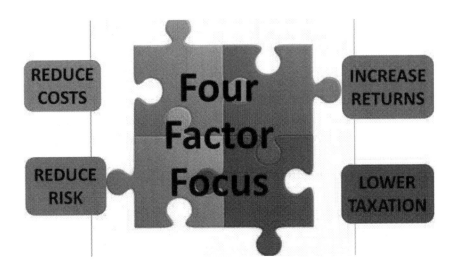

Here, I explain what each segment incorporates.

Reducing costs
We've already looked within this book at the implications of charges on investments. Hopefully, this has left you feeling better educated to not only ask about what annual management charges are but to ask what the total expense ratio is upon an investment, known as the TER.

The TER can vary hugely as we have already demonstrated but it is imperative that we look to reduce costs as simply 1% on an investment over a lifetime can make a huge impact to our funds.

Reducing Risk
Reducing Risk is to ensure that we understand all risks associated with investments, not only the equity risk of the markets moving up and down but also other risks such as currency risk.

If we are investing in overseas investments, investing in a different currency, i.e. we are investing in pounds, but the underlying fund is invested in euros or dollars or yen, that when the money comes back to the UK, currency fluctuations could have a major implication, either for or against us. It is just another risk we should be aware of.

When we are investing, we need to be sure the levels of risk are comfortable to us. We need to remember it is our money, not the fund manager's money. We need to ensure that the fund manager is aligned with our values and our core beliefs.

If we have a timescale of say 5 to 10 years on our investment as we are coming into retirement and the fund managers general approach is a 20-year term, the levels of risk that they will be taking with our money will not be appropriate for us.

Increasing returns
Many people seem to think that the more risk I take, the more money I will make, this isn't necessarily the case, as the more risk you take, the more money you can lose.
We need to look at how we can diversify our portfolios to help to offset markets when they are going against us, and this counterbalance can ultimately help with active management to increase the returns.

There has been a big drive towards index tracking funds over recent years. Index tracking funds are very inexpensive funds and are wonderful in an up-market. It's like driving a powerful car in a straight line, but when you come to the corners, you need some brakes. That is what active management would do for you.

Lower taxation

Lowering taxation is important. We need to make sure we fully utilise all of our tax-free allowances for investments. Here in the United Kingdom, an Individual Savings Accounts (AKA ISA) is an excellent way to be able to place £20,000* each tax year in a very tax effective manner.

This will allow you to have future growth without capital gains and future income without income tax. Over the next twenty years, you could build yourself a portfolio of approximately £500k-£700k in ISAs; this would be an extremely beneficial approach to retirement, taking into account taxation, as taxation can have a huge impact upon your portfolio.

Figures correct at time of writing. £20,000 for 2018/2019 tax year.

Within our company, we meet the aim of our Four Factor Focus by using an array of the services we have to offer. These include Charge Comparison, Risk Ladder, Our Model Portfolio and The Money Label.

To meet the aim of our Four Factor Focus we used:

    Charge Comparison
getting value for money

     Model Portfolio
24/7 investment advice

     Risk Ladder
understanding risk

     Money Label
understanding money

The Charge Comparison

The Charge Comparison service allows us to constantly review the charges of all investment companies across the UK. If we have noticed that companies are increasing their charges, we can switch, free of charge, to an alternative portfolio.

The Risk Ladder

The Risk Ladder is a simple way to understand Risk and to help our clients reduce the risk of their portfolio so that they are aligned with their own individual requirements.

Our Model Portfolios

These are ten portfolios, either income or growth based, or a combination of both, that allow you to diversify across multiple asset classes and multiple companies all in one place.

The Money Label

This is a tool that we have developed over the years to enable us to look inside the investment companies to check where they are investing, the asset classes and the underlying funds they are investing in and also to identify when companies change their approach or significantly change risk levels.

Over recent years, we have seen some companies who have started to invest in asset-backed mortgage security style investments, loading their funds up to almost 50%. This would be an investment area we would all steer clear of as ultimately it is invested in sub-prime mortgages.

In summary, the Four Factor Focus is always a good mantra for any investor going forward.

Chapter 8
Fear of Missing Out (FOMO)

Another culprit is human nature. As you and I both know, we're emotional creatures with a gift for doing crazy stuff under the influence of emotions such as fear and greed.

Emotions get a hold of us, and we, as investors, tend to do stupid things. For example, we tend to put money into the market and take it out at exactly the wrong time.

You probably know people who got carried away during a bull market and took reckless risks with money they couldn't afford to lose. It's called FOMO. Fear of missing out.

You may also know people who got scared and sold all their stocks in 2008 only to miss out on huge gains when the market rebounded in 2009.

Emotional Behaviour Problems

- Trying to beat market – Buy High Sell Low
- Panicking during volatility selling, taking losses, sitting on side lines missing the upside.
- Putting the eggs in one basket or with exit charges?
- Attachment to long-standing investments

You're never going to earn your way to financial freedom. The real route to riches is to set aside a portion of your money and invest it so that it compounds over many years.

That's how you make your money your slave instead of being a slave to money.

That's how you achieve financial freedom.

Chapter 9
Sequence of returns risk

If you have you ever heard of pound cost averaging then you should be somewhat familiar with sequence of returns risk because it is pound cost averaging's evil twin brother.

Table showing Pound Cost Averaging

Investment	Unit Price	Units
£100	£1.00	100
£100	£0.95	105
£100	£0.90	111
£100	£0.80	125
£100	£0.90	111
£100	£0.95	105
£100	£1.00	100
£700	£1.00	757

Table one shows if you paid in £100 per month into an investment in a falling market, even though the unit price never gained one penny, overall you brought more units and when the unit price recovered it allowed you to make a gain of 8% when the market never made a gain. That's like magic.

Table showing Sequence of Returns Risk

Taking Income	Unit Price	Units
£100	£1.00	100
£100	£0.95	105
£100	£0.90	111
£100	£0.80	125
£100	£0.90	111
£100	£0.95	105
£100	£1.00	100
£700	£1.00	757

However, table two represents the evil twin brother. When you take income from the same scenario, it makes a loss of 8% instead of a gain. Definitely not magic!

Sequence of Returns Risk (or timing of returns risk) describes risks associated with investing and withdrawing money at a point when the balance is down due to investment performance.

This hazard can be created because of a combination of market risk, interest rate risk, and a person's need for money sooner rather than later.

This need is due to two things:
- Anticipated income needs: most commonly, people who are retired must draw out assets as income for their living expenses.
- Unexpected income or withdrawal needs: something unforeseen comes up. Life gets in the way. Perhaps the retiree needs to help a family member or friend, or there's a serious health issue that must be handled.

These two reasons for withdrawing money in the short-term can affect virtually all retirees to varying degrees.

Your portfolio can suffer serious harm because you have to make withdrawals whether you want to or not, regardless of the market conditions at the time. Let's explore how this plays out by considering two investment situations: one during the time of savings and the other during a period of withdrawals.

Example 1: Accumulation for ten years with no withdrawals

The following charts show what can happen to a £100,000 deposit during a hypothetical ten-year period of savings.

	Mrs Jones		
Year	Rate of Return	Annual Gain/Loss	Ending Value
1	30%	£30,000	£130,000
2	20%	£26,000	£156,000
3	10%	£15,600	£171,000
4	10%	£17,160	£188,760
5	10%	£18,876	£207,636
6	10%	£20,764	£228,400
7	10%	£22,840	£251,240
8	10%	£25,124	£276,364
9	-20%	£-55,273	£221,091
10	-30%	£-66,327	£154,764

Returns listed are not typical and are for illustrative purposes only.

	Mr Jones		
Year	Rate of return	Annual Gain/Loss	Ending Value
1	-30%	£-30,000	£70,000
2	-20%	£-14,000	£56,000
3	10%	£5,600	£61,600
4	10%	£6,160	£67,760
5	10%	£6,776	£74,536
6	10%	£7,454	£81,989
7	10%	£8,199	£90,188
8	10%	£9,019	£99,207
9	20%	£19,841	£119,048
10	30%	£35,715	£154,764

Returns listed are not typical and are for illustrative purposes only.

On the first chart (Mrs Jones' deposit), there was a 30% gain in the first year, bumping up the balance to £130,000. The second year saw another gain, this time of 20%, followed by six straight years of positive returns of 10% each. Mrs Jones closed her investment cycle with losses of 20% and 30% in years nine and ten, finishing with a balance of £154,764. This is an example of positive returns early in the savings cycle with a loss at the end.

The opposite happens on the second chart. Mr Jones took a loss of 30% the first year, reducing his £100,000 investment to £70,000. The second year he saw a 20% loss, bringing his balance down to £56,000. That was followed by six straight years of positive returns at 10% each, and then a positive run-up of 20% and 30% in years nine and ten. This illustrates an example of negative returns early in the cycle with a rebound at the end. Interestingly, Mr Jones' ending balance is the same as Mrs Jones': £154,764.

Both investors ended up with the same amount of money regardless of whether the up and down years occurred early or late in the investment cycle. Both experienced a 6% average rate of return because the positives and negatives cancelled each other out, leaving 6 years of 10% returns (60% divided by ten years equals 6%). Again, this is during ten years of savings. No withdrawals were made during this time.

Now, let's see what happens to these hypothetical £100,000 deposits during the same hypothetical ten-year period when Mrs Jones and Mr Jones were making withdrawals for income rather than just saving.

Example 2: Distribution for ten years with withdrawals

		Mrs Jones		
Year	Rate of Return	Beginning value	Withdrawal	Ending Value
		£100,000		
1	30%	£130,000	£6,000	£124,000
2	20%	£148,800	£6,000	£142,800
3	10%	£157,080	£6,000	£151,080
4	10%	£166,188	£6,000	£160,188
5	10%	£176,207	£6,000	£170,207
6	10%	£187,227	£6,000	£181,227
7	10%	£199,350	£6,000	£193,350
8	10%	£212,685	£6,000	£206,685
9	-20%	£165,348	£6,000	£159,348
10	-30%	£111,544	£6,000	£105,544

Mr Jones				
Year	Rate of return	Beginning value	Withdrawal	Ending Value
		£100,00		
1	-30%	£70,000	£6,000	£64,000
2	-20%	£51,200	£6,000	£45,200
3	10%	£49,720	£6,000	£43,720
4	10%	£48,092	£6,000	£42,092
5	10%	£46301	£6,000	£40,301
6	10%	£44,331	£6,000	£38,331
7	10%	£42,164	£6,000	£36,164
8	10%	£39,781	£6,000	£33,781
9	20%	£40,537	£6,000	£34,537
10	20%	£44,898	£6,000	£38,898

Both examples show the same ten-year average rate of return (6%) but with a new wrinkle: 6% of the initial principal balance is being withdrawn per year for retirement income.

For Mr Jones, again there were down years early on but in the late years a rally. The same 10% returns existed for the six years in the middle, giving an average return of 6%.

For Mrs Jones, the reverse happened – positive years early and then negative years later. But look at the difference between the ending balances. Even though 6% of the initial principal balance was withdrawn per year and experience the exact same 6% average rate of return in both examples, Mrs Jones finishes with £105, 544 whilst Mr Jones finishes with only £38, 898.

This is because Mrs Jones made gains early in the investment cycle on a larger balance and her losses on a smaller balance. At the end of a period of years when the two investments seemed to average out the same, Mr Jones was left with fewer assets because his losses were taken against the larger balance and the gains were made against the smaller one.

Therefore, Mr Jones, with the early drop, ended with a drastically lower balance than Mrs Jones, even though they both had the exact same average rate of returns and withdrawals.

Investors speak a lot about returns, but as these examples show, just knowing the returns is not enough when you depend on your investment for retirement income.

Once again, the critical thing to understand is that, although two investments might have the same average returns over time during a period of savings, the sequence of the gains and losses during a period of withdrawals can have a large impact on a portfolio's ending value as the amount of money invested in the first place.

It's how the cards come out of the pack. Whether you're lucky or unlucky. So, we need a game plan of how to invest so we don't end up unlucky.

Chapter 10
Diversification: Don't put all your eggs in one basket

How should I invest? Well with property it's all about location, location, location, with investments it's diversification, diversification, diversification.

What most people don't realise is that investment success is largely a matter of smart 'asset allocation' – of knowing precisely how much of your money to put in different asset classes such as stocks, bonds, real estate, gold and cash.

Diversification is perhaps the most obvious and fundamental rule of all. In its essence, it's what almost everyone knows: don't put all your eggs in one basket but there's a difference between knowing what to do and actually doing what you know.

- Diversify across different asset classes – Avoid putting all your money in estate, stocks, bonds, or any single investment class.

- Diversify within asset classes – Don't put all your money in a favourite stock such as Apple, or Barclays, Shell etc

- Diversify across markets, countries and currencies around the world - We live in a global economy, so don't make the mistake of investing solely in your own country.

- Diversify across time – You're never going to know the right time to buy anything. But if you keep adding to your investments systematically over months and years (in other words, pound cost averaging), you'll reduce your risk and increase your returns over time.

The principle itself may be simple, but implementing it is another matter! It requires real expertise to build customised asset allocation, diversifying among different types of investments such as stocks, bonds, estate and 'alternatives'. Diversification does its job in the worst of seasons.

One reason why diversification is so critical is that it protects us from a natural human tendency to stick with whatever we feel we know. Once a person is comfortable with the idea that a particular approach works or that he or she understands it well - it's tempting to become a one-trick pony! As a result, many people end up investing too heavily in one specific area.

An example of good diversification is how we create our portfolios, across multiple asset classes. These are laid out via our risk ladder (overleaf) which helps to educate and understand risk.

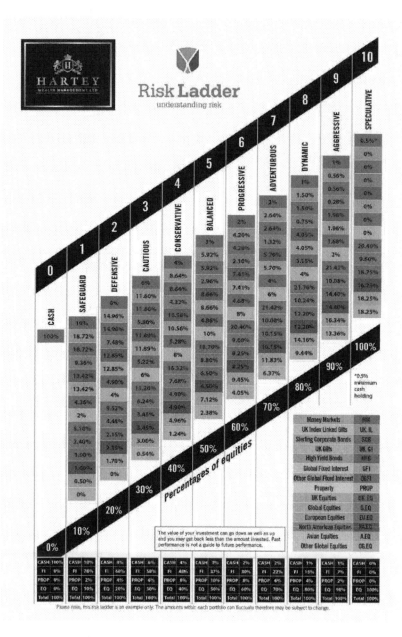

Risk **Ladder**
understanding risk

The value of your investment can go down as well as up and you may get back less than the amount invested. Past performance is not a guide to future performance.

Please note, this risk ladder is an example only. The amounts within each portfolio can fluctuate therefore may be subject to change.

0 CASH

You are not prepared to take any investment risk and it is crucial that your capital is protected. You are prepared to take the inflationary risk this implies with cash investing and accept lower long term returns to meet your risk level.

1 SAFEGUARD

Although a risk averse investor, you are prepared to accept low levels of risk for the prospect of higher returns than cash in the long term. You are not likely to want to invest in equities above a 10% threshold. The vast majority of the portfolio is held in fixed interest with a small property and cash holding to provide some diversification.

2 DEFENSIVE

Although a low risk investor you are comfortable in taking a small amount of investment risk, however capital protection is still fairly important. You are not likely to want to invest in equities above a 20% threshold. The vast majority is held in fixed interest with a small holding in property and cash. The range of assets provides diversification to reduce the overall risk.

3 CAUTIOUS

Although a cautious investor, you are prepared to accept low levels of risk for the prospect of slightly higher returns, but would still like to ensure that capital protection is considered. You are not likely to want to invest in equities above a 30% threshold. The majority is held in fixed interest with a small holding in property and cash. The range of assets provides diversification to reduce the overall risk.

4 CONSERVATIVE

Although a fairly cautious investor, you are prepared to accept a reasonable level of risk for the prospect of more attractive potential returns, but would still like to ensure that capital protection is considered. You are not likely to want to invest in equities above a 40% threshold. Almost half of the portfolio is held in Fixed Interest, with the balanced in property and a small holding in cash. The range of assets provides diversification to reduce the overall risk.

5 BALANCED

You prefer a balanced approach to investment and are willing to accept medium risk in the hope of higher returns. Equities are the majority holding at a 50% threshold with fixed interest representing just in excess of a third of the portfolio with the remainder held in property and a small cash presence. The range of assets provides diversification benefits.

6 PROGRESSIVE

You are comfortable in taking a reasonable amount of risk in order to increase the chance of achieving a better return. Capital protection is less important to you than the return on the investment. Equities are the majority (60%) holding, with Fixed interest, Property representing the remaining balance, with a very small cash holding (2%). The range of assets provides diversification benefits.

7 ADVENTUROUS

You are prepared to take risk with your investment in return for the prospect of the improving longer term investment performance as short term capital protection is not important. You are likely to want to invest in equities as the majority (70%) of your holding, with a fifth of the portfolio held in fixed interest and the remainder in property, with a very small holding (2%). The range of assets provides diversification benefits.

8 DYNAMIC

You will accept a higher than average risk for the prospect of high returns. You are not concerned with short term volatility as your investments may fluctuate in value and you may get back less than you invest. You are likely to want to invest in equities as the vast majority (80%) of your holding, with the remainder is held in fixed interest and property with a very small cash holding (1%) to provide some diversification.

9 AGGRESSIVE

This category is reserved for those investors who are prepared to take high levels of risk in order to obtain the potential for substantial returns, although substantial falls in value may be equally as likely and you may get back less than you invest. You are likely to want to invest in equities for the vast majority (90%) of your holding, with the remainder invested in fixed interest and property in equal measures and a very small cash holding (1%).

10 SPECULATIVE

This category is reserved for those investors who are prepared to take the highest of investment risks in order to obtain the potential for substantial returns, although substantial falls in value may be equally as likely and you may get back less than you invest. You are likely to want to solely invest in equities for the full allocation (100%) and concentration risk may also create high level value swings.

 Chester Office: Hilliards Court, Chester Business Park, Chester, CH4 9PQ
Oswestry Office: 9-11 Salop Road , Oswestry, Shropshire, SY11 2NR
www.harteywm.co.uk **Email:** info@harteywm.co.uk **Freephone:** 0808 168 5866

Registered in England and Wales No: 8288660. Hilliards Court, Chester Business Park, Chester, CH4 9PQ.
Hartey Wealth Management Ltd is authorised and regulated by the Financial Conduct Authority.

Name	Original %
UK Equities	17.91
Global Fixed Interest	15.86
North American Equities	10.91
European Equities	9.01
Property	8.83
UK Gilts	8.75
UK Fixed Interest	7.86
Money Market	5.72
Asia Pacific Emerging Equities	5.62
Others	9.53

Name	Original %
Industrials	14.34
Government Bonds	13.20
Financials	13.02
Telecom, Media & Technology	9.55
Undisclosed	8.66
Consumer Products	7.19
Money Market	5.23
Basic Materials	4.79
Health Care	3.60
Others	20.40

Name	Original %
UK	37.35
North America	17.61
Europe ex UK	17.43
Pacific Basin	7.83
Money Market	5.78
Americas	2.98
Undisclosed	2.96
Asia Pacific	1.73
Australasia	1.69
Other	4.63

Chapter 11

How to save

Firstly, you've got to save and invest – become an owner, not just a consumer. Pay yourself first by taking a percentage of your income and having it automatically deducted from your bank account.

It's time to give yourself a raise: increase what you save from 10% of your income to 15% or from 15% to 20%.

So, now that you've saved it, where are you going to invest for maximum returns so that you reach your target faster?

The single best place to compound your money over many years is in the stock market. A diversified portfolio that includes other assets too is key.

But for now, we're going to focus on the stock market. Why? Because this is incredibly fertile land! Like our ancestors, we need to plant our seeds where we can reap the greatest harvest.

On average, corrections have occurred about once a year since 1990.

Have you ever listened to pundits talking about the stock market and how dramatic they can make it sound?

All they talk about is volatility and turmoil because fear draws you into their programming. The crisis in question might be unrest in the Middle East, slumping oil prices, the downgrading of US debt, a 'fiscal cliff', a budget off, Brexit, a China slowdown or whatever else they can milk for excitement.

The trouble is all this babble, all this drama, all this emotion can make it hard for us to think clearly. Instead of getting distracted by all this noise, it helps to focus on a few key facts that truly matter.

For example, on average, there's been a market correction every year since 1990.

Just think about it; if you're 50 years old today and have a life expectancy of 85, you can expect to live through another 35 corrections.

It shows you that corrections are just a routine part of the game. Instead of living in fear of them you and I have to accept them as regular occurrences – like Spring, Summer, Autumn and Winter.

The average correction ordinarily lasts only 54 days – less than two months! In other words, most corrections are over almost before you know it.

Less than 20% of All Corrections Turn into A Bear Market

When the market starts tumbling – especially when it's down more than 10% many people hit their pain threshold and start to sell because they're scared that this drop could turn into a death spiral.

Aren't they just being sensible and prudent? Actually, not so much. It turns out that fewer than one in five corrections escalates to the point where they become a bear market. To put it another way, 80% of corrections don't turn into bear markets.

Nobody Can Predict Consistently Whether the Market Will Rise or Fall

The media perpetuates a myth that, if you're smart enough, you can predict the market's moves and avoids its downdrafts.
The financial industry sells the same fantasy: big banks confidently predict as if they have a crystal ball or (equally unlikely) superior insight.

Many of them make the same dire predictions every year until they're occasionally right, as anyone would be. After all, even a man with a broken watch can tell you the correct time twice a day.

The fact is, nobody can consistently predict whether markets will rise or fall. It's delusional to think that you or I could successfully 'time the market' by jumping in and out at the right moments.

The stock market rises over time despite many short-term setbacks.

Historically, Bear Markets Have Happened Every Three to Five Years

You're starting to see why it's a good idea to be a long-term investor in the stock market and not merely a short-term trader. It's now equally obvious that you don't need to live in fear of corrections.

You now know that corrections happen regularly and that no one can predict when they will happen and that the market usually rebounds quickly; resuming its general upward trajectory.

But what about bear markets? Should we be terrified of them? We need to understand a few key facts.

The first fact you need to know is that there are 34 bear markets in 115 years between 1900 and 2015. In other words, on average, they happened nearly once every three years.

More recently, bear markets have occurred slightly less often; in the 70 years since 1946, there have been 14 of them. That's a rate of one bear market every five years.
So, depending on when we start counting, it's fair to say that bear markets have historically happened every three to five years.

How Bad Does It Get When the Market Really Crashes?

The FTSE 100 index plunged by more than 40%. If you're someone who panics, sells everything in the midst of this mayhem, and locks in a loss of more than 40%, you're going to feel like a grizzly bear mauled you for real.

Even if you have the knowledge and fortitude not to sell, you'll likely find that bear markets are a gut-wrenching experience.

Sadly, many advisers fall victim to the same fear and hide under their desks during these tumultuous times. Ongoing communication during these storms is the proverbial lighthouse, broadcasting the message 'Stay the course!'

What you need to know; bear markets don't last!

Bear Markets Become Bull Markets, and Pessimism Becomes Optimism

Do you remember how fragile the world seemed in 2008 when banks were collapsing and the stock market was in free fall? When you pictured the future, did it seem dark and dangerous?

Or did it seem like the good times were just around the corner and the party was about to begin?

As you can see from the chart on the below, the market finally hit rock bottom on March 9, 2009. Do you know what happened next?

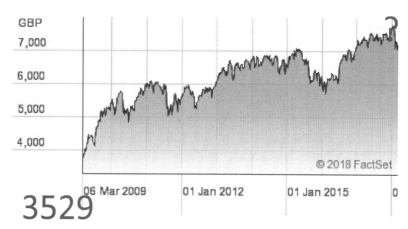

GBP
7,000
6,000
5,000
4,000

© 2018 FactSet

06 Mar 2009   01 Jan 2012   01 Jan 2015   0

3529

Fear

If you live in fear, you've lost the game before its even started. How can you achieve anything if you're too scared to take a risk?

As Shakespeare wrote four centuries ago, "Cowards die many times before their deaths; the valiant never taste death but once."

"Risk comes from not knowing what you're doing."

There's one thing we do know for sure; there will be market crashes in the future, just as there were in the past. But does it make sense to be paralysed with fear merely because there's a risk of getting hurt?

When the next bear market comes, and others are overwhelmed with fear.

In the face of uncertainty will bring you tremendous financial rewards.

In fact, while others live in terror of bear markets, you'll discover they are the single greatest opportunity for building wealth in your lifetime.

Why? Because that's when everything goes on sale. Imagine longing to own a Ferrari and discovering that you can buy one for half price.

Yet when the stock market goes on sale, most people react as if it's a disaster.

You need to understand that bear markets are here to serve you. If you keep your cool, they will actually accelerate your journey to financial freedom. If you find internal certainty, you'll actually be excited when the market crashes.

The Eye of The Storm

In September 2008, the Dow Jones Industrial Average plunged 777 points. It was the biggest one day drop ever, obliterating $1.2 trillion in wealth.

That same day, the VIX index, a barometer of fear among investors, hit its highest level in history. By March 2009 the market had tumbled more than 50%, devastated by the worst financial crisis since the Great Depression.

This was the perfect storm. Banks collapsed. High-flying funds blew up and crashed to the ground. Some of Wall Streets most renowned investors saw their reputations shattered.

Yet I look back on that tumultuous time as one of the highlights of my career – a time when my wealth management firm, guided its clients to safety, positioning them, so they not only survived the crash but also benefited enormously from the rebound that followed.

If you make the wrong decisions, as most people did in 2008 and 2009, it can be financially catastrophic, setting you back years or even decades. But if you make the right decisions, as my firm and its clients did, then you have nothing to fear.

You'll even learn to welcome bear markets because of the unparalleled opportunities they create for coolheaded bargain hunters.

How did our ship survive the storm while many others sank to the bottom of the sea?

First of all, we were in the better ship! Long before the bear market occurred, we prepared for it in the knowledge that blue skies never last, that hurricanes are inevitable.

None of us knows when a bear market will come, how bad it will be or how long it will last. They've occurred, on average, every three years over the last 115 years.

That's not a reason to hide in terror. It's a reason to ensure that your vessel is safe and seaworthy, regardless of conditions.

There are two primary ways to prepare for market turmoil. First, you need the right asset allocation – a fancy term for the proportion of your portfolio that's invested in different types of assets including stocks, bonds, estate, and alternative investments.

Second, you need to be positioned conservatively enough (with some income set aside for a very rainy day), so that you won't be forced to sell while stocks are down.

It's the financial equivalent of making sure you're equipped with safety harnesses, life vests, and sufficient food before heading out to sea.

As I see it, 90% of surviving a bear market comes down to preparation.

What's the other 10%? That's all about how you react emotionally in the midst of the storm.

That's one reason why having a battle-hardened financial adviser can be helpful.

It provides an emotional ballast, helping you remain calm, so you don't waver at the worst moment and jump overboard!

One advantage our clients had is that we'd gone to great lengths to educate them in advance, so they wouldn't be in shock when a crash occurred.

They understood why they owned what they owned, and they knew these investments were likely to perform in a crash.

It's like being warned by your doctor that a medication might make you dizzy and nauseous; you're not thrilled when this risk becomes a reality, but you'll cope much better than if it were a total surprise.

Even so, some clients needed a lot of reassurance. "Shouldn't we get out of stocks now and go to cash?"

Sir John Templeton's famous remark: "The four most expensive words in investing are "This time it's different."

I kept reminding clients that every bear market has eventually become a bull market, regardless of how bleak the news seemed at the time.

Just think of the many calamities and crises of the twentieth century; can you imagine how investors felt if they'd panicked and sold during those bear markets?

They not only made the disastrous mistake of locking in their losses but missed out on those massive gains as the market revived.

As a financial adviser, I construct a client's portfolio by combining asset classes, each with different risk characteristics and different rates of return.

The goal? To balance the return you need to achieve with the risk you're comfortable taking.

The Greatest Danger Is Being Out of The Market

It's not possible to jump in and out of the market successfully. It's just too difficult for regular mortals like you and me to predict the market's movements.

The idea of a bell ringing to signal when investors should get in or out of the stock market is simply not credible. The trouble is, sitting on the sidelines even for short periods of time may be the costliest mistake of all. I know this sounds counterintuitive.

From 1996 through to 2015, the S&P 500 returned an average of 8.2% a year. But if you missed out on the top 10 trading days during those 20 years, your returns dwindled to just 4.5% a year.

Can you believe it? Your returns would have been cut almost in half just by missing the 10 best trading days in 20 years!
It gets worse! If you missed out on the top 20 trading days, your returns dropped from 8.2% a year to a paltry 2.1%.

And if you missed out on the top 30 trading days, your returns vanished into thin air, falling all the way to 0%!

Meanwhile, a study by JPMorgan found that 6 of the 10 best days in the market over the last 20 years occurred within two weeks of the worst 10 days.

The moral: if you get spooked and sold at the wrong time, you missed out on the fabulous days that followed which is when patient investors made almost all of their profits. In other words, market turmoil isn't something to fear. It's the greatest opportunity for you to leapfrog to financial freedom.

You can't win by sitting on the bench. You have to be on the pitch.

To put it another way, fear isn't rewarded. Courage is.

The truth is, the majority of plans are characterised by huge broker commissions, expensive actively managed funds, and layer after layer of additional and often hidden charges.

We're not referring to absurdly high fees that you're being charged by the mutual funds. It's not enough for you to pay for all those actively managed funds. No these are additional fees that you're also being charged by the plan provider that's administering your money. These providers are typically insurance companies. They're truly ingenious when it comes to dreaming up different ways to syphon off the money. Here's a short example of the many categories of fees they've invented: investment expenses, communication expenses, book-keeping expenses, administrative expenses, trustee expenses, legal expenses, transactional expenses, and stewardship expenses. Why not just add a category called 'expenses expenses'?

Excessive expenses can easily destroy the benefits of all that effort. Some plans take the excessive fees to a whole new level. Certain providers, not content with their typical take, charge a front-end fee on all initial deposits. One of the worst we have seen takes a whopping 5.75% of every single pound you put away. It's like a tithe to the corporate gods running these companies. Add that to the 2% annual fees they charge and you're down 7.75% before you're out of the gate.

That is why it is so important to be aware of how the financial industry stacks the odds against you. Knowledge is your first defence. After all, how can you protect yourself from a threat to your financial well-being unless you know that this threat exists?

Another well-known insurance company charges a 3% sales load to buy a Vanguard index fund and then charges 0.65% a year in fees for the fund – a steal at a mere 1300% mark up.

This is the white-collar equivalent of ruthless mobsters coming around to your small business and hitting you up for protection money. The only justification is that you have money, and they want it.

Chapter 12

Who can you really trust? Not the puppet.

How do you find an adviser you can trust – and who deserves your trust? It's astonishing how many people don't trust the person giving them financial advice.

I have lots of friends and clients in the financial industry, so I'm speaking with first-hand knowledge when I tell you that they – and the vast majority of their colleagues – are people of real integrity. They have good hearts and good intentions.

The trouble is, they work in a system that's beyond their control – a system that has tremendously powerful financial incentives to focus on maximising profits above all else. This is a system that richly rewards employees who put their employer's interests first, their own interests second and their clients' interests a distant third.

And for folks like you and me, that's a recipe for disaster – unless we take the precaution of learning how the system works against us, and how to counter use it.

Before we go any further, it's worth explaining where financial advisers fit within this profit-hungry system – and what exactly they do.

They operate in a realm where nothing is quite what it seems to be. So, it's fitting that they go by many different names, which often seem downright misleading.

Different designations for financial advisers including 'financial consultants', 'wealth managers', 'financial advisers', 'investment consultants', 'wealth advisers' and (in case that doesn't sound exclusive enough) 'private wealth advisers'. These are all just different ways of saying 'I'm respectable! I'm professional! Of course you can trust me!

Regardless of the title, what you really need to know is who are truly independent advisers and not those working for a bank, a building society, or an adviser who is restricted in the products he can recommend.

It's also key to know the advisers that are independent but are owned by an insurance company as there is a huge conflict of interest. They are under immense pressure to sell the company's products, and now we see consolidating companies buying up independents simply to hoover up money to put on their DFM platforms.

Buyer be aware

Those tied advisers are paid to sell financial products to customers like you in return for a a fat commission.

Because the salesperson has a vested interest in hawking expensive products, which might include actively managed mutual funds, whole life insurance policies, variable annuities, and wrap accounts.

These products typically pay them a onetime sales commission or even better for them, ongoing annual fees. Along with being required to produce sales targets to qualify for the annual sales convention in Barbados or a nice cruise.

So, it doesn't matter how fancy the title sounds: these are salespeople under intense pressure to generate revenues.

If calling themselves a financial consultant or a private wealth adviser helps them reach their aggressive sales targets, so be it. If calling themselves a wizard, a pixie, or an elf helped more, that'd be fine too.

Does this mean they're dishonest?

Not at all. But it does mean they're working for the house. And remember; the house always wins.

There's a good chance your adviser is a sincere person with high integrity, but he's selling what he's been trained to sell – and you should always assume that whatever he's selling will benefit the house first.

They're not evil or malicious. They never set out to sabotage the global economic system!

These companies simply do what they're incentivised to do, which is to meet shareholders' needs. And what do shareholders need? Bigger profits. And what creates bigger profits? More fees.

If there's a legally grey area that these companies can exploit to generate those additional fees, they're likely to do it because that what they're incentivised to do.

Maybe you're wondering if you need an adviser at all. But in my experience, the best financial advisers can add extraordinary value by helping you with everything from investing, to taxes, to insurance.

They provide holistic advice that's truly invaluable.

While wrong advisers can be detrimental to your financial health, the right ones can be worth their value in gold

How can you tell if the person offering you help is the real deal?

And how can you even know where to start, when so many different people with so many different titles are offering you potential solutions?

In the interests of cutting through confusion, I'm going to make this as simple and straightforward as possible. In reality, all financial advisers fall into just one of three categories:

- Tied to one company
- An independent adviser (whole of market)
- A restricted adviser

How do you know if the product the tied adviser or restricted adviser recommends is the best one for you?

Let me clear it up. They don't recommend the best product for you.

All they're obliged to do is follow what's known as the 'suitability' standard. That means they must simply believe any recommendations they make are 'suitable' for their clients.

Suitability is an extremely low bar to clear.

The problem is, these advisers and their employees earn more by recommending certain products. For example, an actively managed fund with high expenses will be far more lucrative for the adviser than a low-cost index fund, which will be far more lucrative for you and your family.

Does it sound to you like there's a serious conflict of interest here?

How is it that profits over people has become the accepted standard?

To put this in context, the United Kingdom has a fiduciary standard, which means all financial advisers are required by law to act in their client's best interest

There have been many attempts to enact laws requiring advisers to serve their clients best interests.

The Financial Conduct Authority's principles of good regulation:

1. Recognising the differences in the businesses carried on by different regulated persons
Where appropriate, we exercise our functions in a way that recognises differences in the nature of, and objectives of, businesses carried on by different persons subject to requirements imposed by or under FSMA.

2. Openness and disclosure
We should publish relevant market information about regulated persons or require them to publish it (with appropriate safeguards). This reinforces market discipline and improves consumers' knowledge about their financial matters.

3. Transparency
We should exercise our functions as transparently as possible. It is important that we provide appropriate information on our regulatory decisions, and that we are open and accessible to the regulated community and the general public.

The principles for businesses:

4. Integrity
A firm must conduct its business with integrity.

5. Skill, care and diligence
A firm must conduct its business with due skill, care and diligence.

6. Management and control
A firm must take reasonable care to organise and control its affairs responsibly and effectively, with adequate risk management systems.

7. Financial prudence
A firm must maintain adequate financial resources.

8. Market conduct
A firm must observe proper standards of market conduct.

9. Customers' interests
A firm must pay due regard to the interests of its customers and treat them fairly.

10. Communications with clients
A firm must pay due regard to the information needs of its clients and communicate information to them in a way which is clear, fair and not misleading.

11. Conflicts of interest
A firm must manage conflicts of interest fairly, both between itself and its customers and between a customer and another client.

12. Customers: relationships of trust
A firm must take reasonable care to ensure the suitability of its advice and discretionary decisions for any customer who is entitled to rely upon its judgment.

13. Clients' assets

A firm must arrange adequate protection for clients' assets when it is responsible for them.

14. Relations with regulators
A firm must deal with its regulators in an open and cooperative way and must disclose to the appropriate regulator appropriately anything relating to the firm of which that regulator would reasonably expect notice.

Here's the bottom line: this system is so riddled with conflicts of interest that it puts you in a highly vulnerable position. But what if you're already working with a tied or restricted adviser you like and trust?

I'm not suggesting that it's impossible to find talented, trustworthy tied or restricted adviser who do a fine job. But playing a game where the odds are so heavily stacked against you isn't an intelligent move.
Why would you ever choose a financial adviser who doesn't have to act in your best interests over one who does?

You wouldn't! Yet most do just that. One reason is that they simply don't know any better. The fact that you're reading this book puts you in an elite group – one that understands the fundamental rules of this high stakes game.

The poor client pays the adviser twice: for independent advice on which investments to own and for the parent company's own mediocre funds.

Most clients aren't even aware that they're buying funds owned by the same firm. That's because the fund arm and the advisory arm typically operate under different brand names. It's like watching a master pickpocket at work.

An Additional Fee for Doing Nothing

Here's another scheme that's become increasingly common: you pay an adviser a fee to manage your money – let's say 1% of your assets. The adviser then recommends a model portfolio, which has its own additional fee – let's say 0.25% of your assets. This fee is over and above the cost of the underlying investments in your portfolio.

But nothing additional is being done for you: the 'model portfolio' consists of various investments the adviser has assembled, which is what you paid him to do in the first place. It's like buying £100 worth of groceries and then getting slapped with a £25 fee for the right to carry them out of the shop in a paper bag.

If an adviser charges a money management fee for selecting investments, that should be it. End of story.

Why should they be able to add another fee for pooling those investments together?

I'll tell you why: because they can.

Much of the chapter has focused on the hidden fees, smoke and mirrors and where companies use terminology to confuse people, such as there's no exit fee. What they don't tell you is that there is an early withdrawal fee.

You are much better off seeking great independent financial advice.

You:
- Aren't tied
- Aren't restricted
- Do not have advisers selling their own funds
- Do not have advisers with huge conflicts of interest
- Do not have advisers who only sell DFM's without passive funds.

My experience has shown that over three decades that nothing has a positive impact on their financial future than partnering with an intelligent guide who knows the territory and can show you proven ways to win.

A world-class adviser will help you define your goals, keep you on the path towards them and help to weather volatile markets by offering actively managed and passive funds. What's more, they offer conflict-free investment advice that's comprehensive.

You are looking for an independent client-focused adviser who is highly skilled and actively provide the service they claim.

Ask for reviews from their clients to ensure that the promises that were made have been delivered upon.

I was taught four basic skills that have served me well:

- Say Please
- Say Thank You
- Turn up on time
- Do as I say and follow through

How many people do you know who don't do the basics?

Here at Hartey Wealth Management, we have a structured team of experts that our clients have access to. The team includes experts on investing, pensions, mortgages, insurance, estate planning, wills and trusts.

The cost is just 1% per annum of assets held for this entire team of experts.

What is active management?

Actively managed investment funds are run by professional fund managers or investment research teams who make all the investment decisions, such as which companies to invest in or when to buy and sell different assets, on your behalf.

They have extensive access to research in different markets and sectors and often meet with companies to analyse and assess their prospects before making a decision to invest.

The aim of active management is to deliver a return that is superior to the market as a whole or, for funds with more conservative investment strategies, to protect capital and lose less value

If markets fall an actively managed fund can offer you the potential for much higher returns than a market provides if your fund manager makes the right calls.

It also means that you have somebody tactically managing your money, so when a particular sector looks like it might be on the up or one region starts to suffer, the fund manager can move your money accordingly to expose you to this growth or shield you from potential losses.

How does this differ from passive management?

Passive investment funds will simply track a market – and charge far less in comparison. The funds are essentially run by computer and will buy all of the assets in a particular market, or the majority, to give you a return that reflects how the market is performing. **Check out the Advisers credentials.**

You need to make sure that the person, or someone on their team, has the right qualifications for the job you need doing.

We're not talking about fancy titles here; I mean professional credentials.

These credentials aren't a guarantee of high-level skills. Even so, it's important to know that any adviser you're considering has reached the minimum level of competency required to advise in the relevant field.

Ideally, if you're using an adviser, you should be getting more than just someone to design your investment strategy.

What you really need is someone who can help you as the years go by to grow your overall wealth by showing you how to save money on your mortgage, insurance, taxes, and so on – someone who can also help you design and protect your legacy.

That might sound unnecessary right now, but it's important to have this breadth of expertise since taxes alone can make a difference of 30% to 50% in what you retain from your investments today.

I find it ironic when I see ads for wealth management, and all they're doing is designing a portfolio. It's best to start with a person you're going to grow with through time. So, make sure he has the resources to grow with you even if you're starting small. Also, keep in mind, size does matter. You don't want to end up with a sincere but inexperienced adviser who only manages relatively tiny sums for a few dozen clients.

Next, you want to make sure your adviser has experience in working with people just like you.

Do they have a track record to prove they've performed well for clients in your position, with your needs?

For example, if your main focus is on building wealth so you can retire, you want real experts in retirement planning.

Yet in an anonymous survey, the 'Journal of Financial Planning' found that 46% of advisers had no retirement plan of their own.

I can't believe they admitted this! Can you imagine hiring a personal trainer who hasn't exercised in two decades, or a nutritionist who's scoffing chocolates whilst telling you to eat vegetables?

It's also important to make sure that you and your adviser are aligned philosophically.

Finally, it's important to find an adviser you can relate to on a personal level.

A good adviser will be a partner and ally for many years, guiding you on a long-distance financial journey. Sure, it's a professional relationship, but isn't money also a deeply personal subject for you, or is it just me?

It's tied up with our hopes and dreams, our desire to take care of the next generation, to have a charitable impact, to lead an extraordinary life on our own terms. It helps if you can have these conversations with an adviser you can connect with, trust and like.

Chapter 13
The job interview

Seven key questions to ask any adviser

I always call it the job interview. The adviser is applying for the job of looking after your family and money, not for now but over the years ahead.

The adviser should be interviewing you to check there is a mutual fit, for both parties. The starting point is trust, like and mutual respect.

One way to make sure you hire the right adviser is to ask him or her several questions that will help you to uncover any potential conflicts and concerns that you might miss otherwise.

If you have an adviser already, it's equally important for you to get the answer to these questions. Here's what I'd want to know before placing my financial future in the hands of any adviser:

1. Are you a registered, regulated Investment Adviser?

If the answer is no, smile sweetly and say goodbye.
If the answer is yes, you still need to figure out if the independent is wearing one hat or two.

2. Are you (or your firm) affiliated with an investment company (i.e. a puppet on a string)?

If the answer is yes, you're dealing with someone who is a tied or restricted adviser and usually has an incentive to steer you to specific investments.

One easy way to figure this out is to glance at the bottom of the adviser's website or business card and see if there's a sentence like this: the adviser is an appointed representative of a life assurance/ investment company.

Run for your life!

3. Does your firm offer proprietary mutual funds or separately managed accounts?

You want the answer to be an emphatic no. If the answer is yes, then watch your wallet like a hawk.

It probably means they're looking to generate additional revenues by steering you into these products that are highly profitable for them (but probably not for you).

4. Do you or your firm receive any third-party compensation for recommending particular investments?

This is the ultimate question that you want answering. Why? Because you need to know that your adviser has no incentive to recommend products that will shower him or her with commissions, kickbacks, consulting fees, trips, or other goodies.

5. What's your philosophy when it comes to investing?

This will help you understand whether or not the adviser believes that he or she can beat the market by picking individual stocks or actively managed funds.

6. What financial planning services do you offer beyond investment strategy and portfolio management?

Investment help may be all you need, depending on your stage of life. But as you grow older and/or you become wealthier with various holdings to manage, things often become more complex financially.

For example, you may need to deal with saving for a child's university fees, retirement planning, handling your vested stock options, or estate planning. Most advisers have limited capabilities once they venture beyond investing

7. Where will my money be held? A fiduciary adviser should always use a third-party custodian to hold your funds.

The good news about this arrangement is that if you ever want to fire the adviser, you don't have to move your accounts.

You can simply hire a new adviser who can take over managing your accounts without missing a beat. This custodial system also protects you from the danger of getting fleeced.

Our Investment Process

1 STRUCTURING THE RIGHT PORTFOLIO — Our comprehensive wealth planning process delivers the right mix of assets for your financial goals.

2 DIVERSIFICATION REDUCE RISK EXPOSURE — By investing across asset classes, companies and geography, we achieve the best defence against market uncertainty and risk.

3 PROTECTION FROM INFLATION — To sustain your wealth in the years to come, it is critical that your portfolio can defend your purchasing power against inflation.

4 REDUCE COST GETTING A FAIR PRICE — Managing the costs of your investments will ensure that you get benefits at a fair and competitive price

5 CONTROL EMOTIONAL DECISIONS — Our role is to coach you to avoid 'buy high' and 'sell low' emotional doubts and to provide information and reassurance.

6 REBALANCING YOUR PORTFOLIO — Keeping your original asset mix requires rebalancing on a regular basis to avoid taking on volatility and risk beyond your tolerance.

About Hartey Wealth Management

Multi award-winning Wealth Management Firm, Hartey Wealth Management opened their doors in 2014.

The vision of the company was to adopt a totally fresh client first approach whilst drawing on the adviser's twenty-five plus years of experience running a regional business, providing clients with the very best unbiased, independent financial advice.

Hartey Wealth Management's fierce commitment to independence means there are no hidden fees or commissions, no external shareholders and no bias to any retail providers to cloud our vision or promote conflicts of interest. We are singularly focused on providing advice and solutions that champion our clients' best interests.

As such we're putting our future success in the hands of our clients. We've turned our backs on the typical commission you would receive from ordinary insurance companies and have chosen to sit on the same side of the desk as our clients to represent them rather than be the middleman. We aim to keep things fair and let our clients simply pay our fee only, not those of us and others too.

Our trademarked Second Opinion Service – a service which provides a completely unbiased opinion on the investments, pensions and finances of clients and prospective clients, giving them a greater insight and understanding of how they are performing and whether they are making the right decisions – ensures our clients are taken on a thorough journey, allowing them to consider the improvements we could make to their risk levels, their charges and their investment performance.

Our relationships with our clients are thriving, and as such we're successfully achieving consistent 5* reviews based on our integrity, honesty and knowledge.

We know getting financial advice isn't a decision to be taken lightly, so it's important we're on hand to offer a professional, clear and tailored service. The awards we've won are a huge achievement, and I'm delighted that our hard work and commitment to our clients is being recognised. We'd like to thank our clients for their support over the past few years as without them we wouldn't be where we are today. We're looking forward to many more successful years to come.

Our Strategic Approach to Investing

Providing investment advice can be complex and difficult and difficult to interpret. We offer a five-step process to help you understand the compliant investment process that you are about to embark upon, allowing you to measure your progress on your financial journey.

5. Fact Find
We begin by getting to know you and establish your goals and expectations.

4. Rigorous Risk Assessment
We provide regular reviews and reports on your investments and automatically rebalance portfolios to ensure the very best performance.

3. Risk assessment discussion
It is important to discuss and understand what the risk score means and whether it accurately matches your true attitude to risk and loss.

2. Tailored to match our model portfolios
We match you to one of our 10 model portfolios, designed to provide maximum returns for your given level of risk.

1. Review, reporting and rebalancing

Our Risk Profile Questionnaire helps to meet our clients' expectations with far greater precision.

The
process of effective financial management involves understanding an investor's attitude to risk and then choosing a spread of investments to match it. This requires access to a range of world-class investment, with the flexibility to refine the investment choices as the needs of the investor changes.

About Karl Hartey

Karl has been working in the realms of financial advice for over 30 years, building solid relationships with clients. Following a short break from advising, Karl and Tristan opened Hartey Wealth Management in 2014. As well as advising Karl brings a whole host of wisdom, knowledge and experience to each and every area of the company and is constantly driving positive changes to improve the service we are offering. He has successfully lead the company to win multiple awards over the last few years.

As well as hosting a number of our very own events, Karl has been invited to be a main platform speaker at the prestigious Million Dollar Round Table Conference in front of thousands of global advisers, along with speaking at multiple international conferences. He has also written two other books; Consider, Decide, Act and Educate My Money, which help to explain the muddled world of finance and its products.

Outside of work, Karl is a keen mountain biker spending much of his spare time on bike tracks and trails. Alongside this, he thrives on travel and adventures and has taken part in over ten international car rallies around the world. Karl is also a patron of the Charlotte Hartey Foundation, a charity which is focused on helping children.

Glossary of Financial Terms

Alpha
Alpha is a measure of a fund's over or under performance compared to its benchmark. It represents the return of the fund when the benchmark is assumed to have a return of zero. It shows the extra value that the manager's activities seem to have contributed. If the Alpha is 5, the fund has outperformed its benchmark by 5% and the greater the Alpha, the greater the outperformance.

Alternative Assets
Includes private real estate, public real estate, venture capital, non-venture private equity, hedge funds, distressed securities, oil and gas partnerships, event arbitrage, general arbitrage, managed funds, commodities, timber and other.

American Stock Exchange
AMEX is the second-largest stock exchange in the U.S., after the New York Stock Exchange (NYSE). In general, the listing rules are a little more lenient than those of the NYSE, and thus the AMEX has a larger representation of stocks and bonds issued by smaller companies than the NYSE. Some index options and interest rate options trading also occur on the AMEX. The AMEX started as an alternative to the NYSE. It originated when brokers began meeting on the curb outside the NYSE in order to trade stocks that failed to meet the Big Board's stringent listing requirements, but the AMEX now has its own trading floor. In 1998, the

parent company of the NASDAQ purchased the AMEX and combined their markets, although the two continue to operate separately. Also called The Curb.

Annual Rate of Return
There are several ways of calculating this. The most commonly used methodologies reflect the compounding effect of each period's increase or decrease from the previous period.

Annual Percentage Rate (APR)
The APR is designed to measure the "true cost of a loan". The aim is to create a level playing field for lenders preventing them from advertising a low rate and hiding fees. In the case of a mortgage, the APR should reflect the yearly cost of a mortgage, including interest, mortgage insurance, and the origination fee, expressed as a percentage.

Annual Premium Equivalent
Calculated as regular premiums plus 10% of single premiums.

Arbitrage
A financial transaction or strategy that seeks to profit from a price differential perceived with respect to related or correlated instruments in different markets. Typically involves the simultaneous purchase of an instrument in one market and the sale of the same or related instrument in another market.

Asset Allocation
Apportioning of investment funds among categories of assets such as cash equivalents, stock, fixed-income investments, alternative investments such as hedge funds and managed futures funds, and tangible assets like real estate, precious metals and collectibles.

Average Monthly Gain
The average of all the profitable months of the fund.

Average Monthly Loss
The average of all the negative months of the fund.

Average Monthly Return
The average of all the monthly performance numbers of the fund.

B

Basis Point
A basis point is one one-hundredth of a percent, i.e. 50 basis points or "bps" is 0.5%.

Bear / Bear Market
Bear is a term describing an investor who thinks that a market will decline. The term also refers to a short position held by a market maker. A Bear Market is a market where prices are falling over an extended period.

Bellwether
A stock or bond that is widely believed to be an indicator of the overall market's condition. Also known as Barometer stock.

Beta
Beta is a measure of a fund's volatility compared to its benchmark, or how sensitive it is to market movements. A fund with a Beta close to 1 means that the fund will generally move in line with the benchmark. Higher than 1 and the fund is more volatile than the benchmark, so that with a Beta of 1.5, say, the

fund will be expected to rise or fall 1.5 points for every 1 point of benchmark movement. If this Beta is an advantage in a rising market – a 15% gain for every 10% rise in the benchmark –the reverse is true when markets fall. This is when managers will look for Betas below 1 so that in a down market the fund will not perform as badly as its benchmark.

Bid Price
The price at which an investor may sell units of a fund back to the fund manager. It is also the price at which a market maker will buy shares.

Blue Chips
Large, continuously well-performing stock, presumed to be among the safer investments on an exchange.

Bond
A debt investment, with which the investor loans money to an entity (company or Government) that borrows the funds for a defined period of time at a specified interest rate. The indebted entity issues investors a certificate or bond, that states the interest rate (coupon rate) that will be paid and when the loaned funds are to be returned (maturity date). Interest on bonds is usually paid every six months.

Bond Rating Codes

Rating	S&P	Moody's
Highest quality	AAA	Aaa
High quality	AA	Aa
Upper medium quality	A	A
Medium grade	BBB	Baa
Somewhat speculative	BB	Ba
Low grade, speculative	B	B
Low grade, default possible	CCC	Caa
Low grade, partial recovery possible	CC	Ca
Default, recovery unlikely	C	C

Bottom-up Investing

An approach to investing which seeks to identify well-performing individual securities before considering the impact of economic trends.

BRIC

A term used to refer to the combination of Brazil, Russia, India and China. The general consensus is that the term was first prominently used in a thesis of the Goldman Sachs Investment Bank. The main point of this 2003 paper was to argue that the economies of the BRICs are rapidly developing and by the year 2050 will eclipse most of the current richest countries of the world. Due to the popularity of the Goldman Sachs thesis, "BRIC" and "BRIMC" (M for Mexico), these terms are also extended to "BRICS" (S for South Africa) and "BRICKET" (including Eastern Europe and Turkey) and have become more generic terms to refer to these emerging markets.

Bull / Bull Market

An investor who believes that the market is likely to rise. A Bull Market is a market where prices are rising over an extended period.

Bulldog Bond

A sterling denominated bond that is issued in London by a company that is not British. These sterling bonds are referred to as bulldog bonds as the bulldog is a national symbol of England.

C

Child Trust Fund

A Child Trust Fund is a savings and investment account for children. Children born on or after 1st September 2002 will receive a £250 voucher to start their account. The account belongs to the child and can't be touched until they turn 18 so that the child has some money behind them to start their adult life. Payments or contributions can be made up to a maximum of £1,200 per 12-month period (starting on the birthday of the child), excluding the voucher amount. Interest and capital growth will be earned tax-free. Additional deposits can be made by parents, grandparents or anyone else.

Closed-end Fund

A type of fund that has a fixed number of shares or units. Unlike open-ended mutual funds, closed-end funds do not stand ready to issue and redeem shares on a continuous basis.

Collar

A contract that protects the holder from a rise or fall in interest rates or some other underlying security above or below certain fixed points. The contract offers the investor protection from interest rate moves outside of an expected range.

Constant Proportion Portfolio Insurance (CPPI)

A strategy that basically buys shares as they rise and sells shares as they fall. To implement a CPPI strategy, the investor selects a floor below which the portfolio value is not allowed to fall. The floor increases in value at the rate of return on cash. If you think of the difference between the assets and floor as a "cushion", then the CPPI decision rule is to simply keep the exposure to shares a constant multiple of the cushion.

Consumer Discretionary Sector

The array of businesses included in the Consumer Discretionary Sector are categorised into five industry groups. They are Automobiles and Components, Consumer Durables and Apparel, Hotels, Restaurants and Leisure, Media, and Retailing.

Consumer Staples

The industries that manufacture and sell food/beverages, tobacco, prescription drugs and household products. Proctor and Gamble would be considered a consumer staple company because many of its products are household and food related.

Convertible Arbitrage

This is an investment strategy that involves taking a long position on a convertible security and a short position in its converting common stock. This strategy attempts to exploit profits when there is a pricing error made in the conversion factor of the convertible security.

Convertible Bond

A bond that can be exchanged, at the option of the holder, for a specific number of shares of the company's preferred stock or common stock. Convertibility affects the performance of the bond in certain ways.

First and foremost, convertible bonds tend to have lower interest rates than nonconvertible because they also accrue value as the price of the underlying stock rises. In this way, convertible bonds offer some of the benefits of both stocks and bonds.

Convertibles earn interest even when the stock is trading down or sideways, but when the stock prices rise, the value of the convertible increases. Therefore, convertibles can offer protection against a decline in stock price. Because they are sold at a premium over the price of the stock, convertibles should be expected to earn that premium back in the first three or four years after purchase.

Core Fund

A fund that takes a middle of the road approach to generate returns for shareholders. These funds are generally structured in two ways. One strategy is to combine stocks and bonds (and possible income trusts) into a single fund to achieve a steady return and improved asset allocation. The other approach is to combine growth stocks and value stocks to diversify the risk from the typical ups and downs of markets. This type of fund can also be called a blend fund since it can show characteristics of a pure growth fund or a pure value fund. Either way, a core fund is focused to producing long-term results.

Corporate Bonds

Corporate Bonds are similar to gilts but are a form of borrowing by companies rather than governments. Let's say AstraZeneca wished to borrow a billion pounds for research and development. They would initially approach their brokers who would review the strength of AstraZeneca versus the Government to assess what is a reasonable "risk premium". A secure company might be able to borrow money at 1 or 2 percentage points above the gilt rate, and a very insecure company may have to pay 10 percentage points above the Government rate or in some cases substantially more. Companies' security is generally graded from AAA to no rating, the less secure debt being known in the UK as "High Yield", or as it is more accurately described by Americans as "Junk Bonds". So, with Corporate Bonds, the short-term returns will vary in line with interest rates as they do with gilts, but also in line with the perceived strength of the company.

Correlation

A standardised measure of the relative movement between two variables, such as the price of a fund and an index. The degree of correlation between two variables is measured on a scale of −1 to +1. If two variables move up or down together, they are positively correlated. If they tend to move in opposite directions, they are negatively correlated.

Coupon

Denotes the rate of interest on a fixed-interest security. A 10% coupon pays interest of 10% a year on the nominal value of the stock.

Cyclical Stock

The stock of a company which is sensitive to business cycles and whose performance is strongly tied to the overall economy. Cyclical companies tend to make products or provide services that are in lower demand during downturns in the economy and higher demand during upswings. Examples include the automobile, steel, and housing industries. The stock price of a cyclical company will often rise just before an economic upturn begins and fall just before a downturn. Investors in cyclical stocks try to make the largest gains by buying the stock at the bottom of a business cycle, just before a turnaround begins. Opposite of defensive stock.

D

Debenture

A loan raised by a company, paying a fixed rate of interest and secured on the assets of the company.

Defensive Stock

A stock that tends to remain stable under difficult economic conditions. Defensive stocks include food, tobacco, oil, and utilities. These stocks hold up in hard times because demand does not decrease as dramatically as it may in other sectors. Defensive stocks tend to lag behind the rest of the market during economic expansion because demand does not increase as dramatically in an upswing.

Delta

The rate at which the price of an option changes in response to a move in the price of the underlying security. If an option's delta is 0.5 (out of a maximum of 1), a $2 move in the price of the underlying will produce a $1 move in the option.

Delta Hedge
A hedging position that causes a portfolio to be delta neutral.

Derivatives
Financial contracts whose value is tied to an underlying asset. Derivatives include futures and options.

Discount
When a security is selling below its normal market price, opposite of premium.

Distressed Securities
A distressed security is a security of a company which is currently in default, bankruptcy, financial distress or a turnaround situation.

E

Efficient Frontier
A line created from the risk-reward graph, comprised of optimal portfolios. The optimal portfolios plotted along the curve have the highest expected return possible for the given amount of risk.

European Fair-Trade Association (EFTA)
A network of 11 Fair Trade organisations in nine European countries which import Fair Trade products from some 400 economically disadvantaged producer groups in Africa, Asia and Latin America. EFTA's members are based in Austria, Belgium, France, Germany, Italy, the Netherlands, Spain, Switzerland and the United Kingdom.

Embedded Value (EV)
A method of accounting used by a life insurance business. The embedded value is the sum of the net assets of the insurance business under conventional accounting and the present value of the in-force business based on estimates of future cash flows and conservative assumptions about, for example, mortality, persistence and expenses. Accounts users prefer this method because it gives a separate indication of new business profitability, a key performance indicator for a life insurer.

Emerging Markets
Typically includes markets within countries that have an underdeveloped or developing infrastructure with significant potential for economic growth and increased capital market participation for foreign investors.

These countries generally possess some of the following characteristics; per capita GNP less than $9000, recent economic liberalisation, debt ratings below investment grade, recent liberalisation of the political system and non-membership of the Organisation of Economic Cooperation and Development. Because many emerging countries do not allow short selling or offer viable futures or other derivatives products with which to hedge, emerging market investing entails investing in geographic regions that have underdeveloped capital markets and exhibit high growth rates and high rates of inflation.

Investing in emerging markets can be very volatile and may also involve currency risk, political risk and liquidity risk. Generally, a long only investment strategy.

Emerging Markets Debt

Debt instruments of emerging market countries. Most bonds are US Dollar denominated, and a majority of secondary market trading is in Brady bonds.

Equities

Ownership positions in companies that can be traded in public markets. Often produce current income which is paid in the form of quarterly dividends. In the event of the company going bankrupt equity holders' claims are subordinate to the claims of preferred stockholders and bondholders.

Equity Hedge

Also known as long/short equity, combines core long holdings of equities with short sales of stock or stock index options. Equity hedge portfolios may be anywhere from net long to net short depending on market conditions. Equity hedge managers generally increase net long exposure in bull markets and decrease net long exposure or are even net short in a bear market.

Equity Market Neutral

This investment strategy is designed to exploit equity market inefficiencies and usually involves being simultaneously long and short equity portfolios of the same size within a country. Market neutral portfolios are designed to be either beta or currency neutral or both. Attempts are often made to control industry, sector and market capitalisation exposures.

Equity Risk

The risk of owning stock or having some other form of ownership interest.

Ethical Investing
Choosing to invest in companies that operate ethically, provide social benefits, and are sensitive to the environment. Also called socially conscious investing.

EU
The European Union. The economic association of over a dozen European countries which seek to create a unified, barrier-free market for products and services throughout the continent. The majority of countries share a common currency with a unified authority over that currency. Notable exceptions to the common currency are the UK, Sweden, Norway, Denmark.

Eurobond
A bond issued and traded outside the country whose currency it is denominated in, and outside the regulations of a single country; usually a bond issued by a non-European company for sale in Europe. Interest is paid gross.

Eurozone or Euroland
The collective group of countries which use the Euro as their common currency.

Event Driven Investing
Investment strategy seeking to identify and exploit pricing inefficiencies that have been caused by some sort of corporate event such as a merger, spin-off, distressed situation or recapitalisation.

Exit Fee
A fee paid to redeem an investment. It is a charge levied for cashing in a fund's capital.

Exposure
The condition of being subjected to a source of risk.

F

FCP
Fonds Commun de Placement. FCPs are a common fund structure in Luxembourg. In contrast to SICAV, they are not companies, but are organised as co-ownerships and must be managed by a fund management company.

Feeder Fund
A fund which invests only in another fund. The feeder fund may be a different currency to the main fund and may be used to channel cash into the main fund for a different currency class.

Fixed Interest
The term fixed interest is often used by banks and building societies relating to an account that pays a set rate of interest for a set time period. This type of investment is capital secure, and the returns are known at the outset. However, fixed interest within the investment world is a completely different concept. It is used to describe funds that invest in Government Gilts and Corporate Bond securities.

Fixed Income Arbitrage
An investment strategy that seeks to exploit pricing inefficiencies in fixed income securities and their derivative instruments. A typical investment is long, a fixed income security or related instrument that is perceived to be undervalued, and short a similar related fixed income security or related instrument. Often highly leveraged.

Floating Rate

Any interest rate that changes on a periodic basis. The change is usually tied to movement of an outside indicator, such as the Bank of England Base Rate. Movement above or below certain levels is often prevented by a predetermined floor and ceiling for a given rate.

For example, you might see a rate set at "base plus 2%". This means that the rate on the loan will always be 2% higher than the base rate, which changes regularly to take into account changes in the inflation rate. For an individual taking out a loan when rates are low, a fixed rate loan would allow him or her to "lock in" the low rates and not be concerned with fluctuations. On the other hand, if interest rates were historically high at the time of the loan, he or she would benefit from a floating rate loan, because as the prime rate fell to historically normal levels, the rate on the loan would decrease. Also called adjustable rate.

Floor

A contract that protects the holder against a decline in interest rates or prices below a certain point.

Forward

An agreement to execute a transaction at some time in the future. In the foreign exchange market this is a tailor-made deal where an investor agrees to buy or sell an amount of currency at a given date.

Forward Rate Agreement (FRA)

A type of forward contract that is linked to interest rates.

FTSE 100

The Financial Times Stock Exchange 100 stock index, a market cap weighted index of stocks traded on the London Stock Exchange. Similar to the S&P 500 in the United States.

Fund of Funds

An investment vehicle that invests in more than one fund. The portfolio will typically diversify across a variety of investment managers, investment strategies and subcategories. Provides investors with access to managers with higher minimums than individuals might otherwise afford.

Funds under Management

The total amount of funds managed by an entity.

G

Gearing

The effect that borrowing has on the equity capital of a company or the asset value of a fund. If the assets bought with funds borrowed appreciate in value, the excess of value over funds borrowed would accrue to the shareholder, thus augmenting, or gearing up the value of their investment.

Geographic Spread

The distribution in a fund's portfolio over different parts of the world, either by countries or larger areas.

Gilt-Edged Securities

Stocks and shares issued and guaranteed by the British government to raise funds and traded on the Stock Exchange. A relatively risk-free investment, gilts bear fixed interest and are usually redeemable on a specified date. The term is now used generally to describe securities of the highest value. According to the redemption date, gilts are described as short (up to five years), medium, or long (15 years or more).

Gilts

Gilts are effectively Government borrowing. When the Chancellor does not have sufficient income to meet his expenditure, then the Government will often borrow money in the form of gilts. These can be for a variety of different terms, paying a range of interest rates.

A typical example would be a ten-year gilt which may pay, say, 5% income. This is the most secure investment you could buy, as you know the rate of return and you know when you will receive your capital back. The UK Government has never defaulted on a gilt.

If however, you wanted to access your money before maturity then you would have to sell your gilt on the open market. Let's say you were trying to sell your gilt after one year. In order to obtain a value, any potential purchaser will look at the term remaining on your gilt, and the interest rate promised, and compare this to new gilts being launched at the time.

If the Government was then launching a new gilt over a nine-year time period and promising to pay 6% per annum, then clearly nobody is going to want to pay the same amount of money for your gilt which is offering a lower interest rate.

They would probably, therefore, offer at least 9% less than you originally paid for it to reflect the 1% difference in income over the nine years of the remaining term. So, whilst you had set out to achieve guaranteed returns, if you sell a gilt before maturity, you could potentially make a capital loss on it, in this instance a loss of 9% over the year.

However, if you decide to keep the gilt until its maturity, you will still receive all of your interest and the capital back. Having said this, your valuation each year will vary depending on market conditions.

GNMA (Ginnie Mae)
Government National Mortgage Association. A U.S. Government-owned agency which buys mortgages from lending institutions, securitises them and then sells them to investors. Because the payments to investors are guaranteed by the full faith and credit of the U.S. Government, they return slightly less interest than other mortgage-backed securities.

Growth Stocks
The stock of a company which is growing earnings and/or revenue faster than its industry or the overall market. Such companies usually pay little or no dividends, preferring to use the income instead to finance further expansion.

Growth Orientated Portfolios
The dominant theme is growth in revenues, earnings and market share. Many of these portfolios are hedged to mitigate against declines in the overall market.

Global Macro
The investment strategy is based on shifts in global economies. Derivatives are often used to speculate on currency and interest rate movements.

Guided Architecture
In relation to funds, for example, FPIL Premier policyholders may only go into the FPIL mirror fund range – this is guided architecture. In contrast to FPIL Reserve policyholders who may choose any security – open architecture.

H

Hawk
An investor who has a negative view towards inflation and its effects on markets. Hawkish investors prefer higher interest rates in order to maintain reduced inflation.

Hedge
Any transaction with the objective of limiting exposure to risks such as changes in exchange rates or prices.

Hedge Fund
A pooled investment vehicle that is privately organised, administered by investment management professionals and generally not widely available to the general public.

Many hedge funds share a number of characteristics; they hold long and short positions, use leverage to enhance returns, pay performance or incentive fees to their managers, have high minimum investment requirements and target absolute returns.

Generally, hedge funds are not constrained by legal limitations on their investment discretion and can adopt a variety of trading strategies. The hedge fund manager often has its own capital (or that of its principals) invested in the hedge fund it manages.

Herding
Hedge fund managers while taking a position may encourage other investors to follow this trend.

High Conviction Stock Picking
A typical portfolio is not constrained by benchmarks, allowing the manager to pursue an approach where a smaller number of stocks are chosen that may bear little or no resemblance to the consensus view. i.e. the manager's conviction.

High Water Mark
The assurance that a fund only takes fees on profits actually earned by an individual investment. For example, a £10 million investment is made in year one and the fund declines by 50%, leaving £5 million in the fund. In year two, the fund returns 100% bringing the investment value back to £10 million. If a fund has a high water mark, it will not take incentive fees on the return in year two since the investment has never grown. The fund will only take incentive fees if the investment grows above the initial level of £10 million.

High-Yield Bond
Often called junk bonds, these are low grade fixed income securities of companies that show significant upside potential. The bond has to pay a high yield due to significant credit risk.

Hurdle Rate

The minimum investment return a fund must exceed before a performance-based incentive fee can be taken. For example, if a fund has a hurdle rate of 10% and the fund returned 18% for the year, the fund will only take incentive fees on the 8 percentage points above the hurdle rate.

I

Index

An arithmetic mean of selected stocks intended to represent the behaviour of the market or some component of it. One example is the FTSE 100 which adds the current prices of the one hundred FTSE 100 stocks and divides the results by a predetermined number, the divisor.

Index Funds

A fund that attempts to achieve a performance similar to that stated in an index. The purpose of this fund is to realise an investment return at least equal to the broad market covered by the indices while reducing management costs.

Index Linked Gilt

A gilt, the interest and capital of which change in line with the Retail Price Index.

In the Money

A condition where an option has a positive intrinsic value.

Intrinsic Value

A component of the market value of an option. If the strike price of a call option is cheaper than the prevailing market price, then the option has a positive intrinsic value, and is "in the money".

Investment Grade
Something classified as investment grade is, by implication, medium to high quality.
1) In the case of a stock, a firm that has a strong balance sheet, considerable capitalisation, and is recognised as a leader in its industry.
2) In the case of fixed income, a bond with a rating of BBB or higher.

J

January Effect
The tendency of US stock markets to rise between December 31 and the end of the first week in January. The January Effect occurs because many investors choose to sell some of their stock right before the end of the year in order to claim a capital loss for tax purposes. Once the tax calendar rolls over to a new year on January 1st, these same investors quickly reinvest their money in the market, causing stock prices to rise. Although the January Effect has been observed numerous times throughout history, it is difficult for investors to profit from it since the market as a whole expects it to happen and therefore adjusts its prices accordingly.

Junk Bond
A bond that pays a high yield due to significant credit risk.

L

Leverage

When investors borrow funds to increase the amount they have invested in a particular position, they use leverage. Sometimes managers use leverage to enable them to put on new positions without having to take off other positions prematurely. Managers who target very small price discrepancies or spreads will often use leverage to magnify the returns from these discrepancies.

Leverage both magnifies the risk of the strategy as well as creates risk by giving the lender power over the disposition of the investment portfolio. This may occur in the form of increased margin requirements or adverse market shifts, forcing a partial or complete liquidation of the portfolio.

The amount of leverage used by the fund is commonly expressed as a percentage of the fund. For example, if the fund has £1 million and borrows another £2 million to bring the total invested to £3 million, then the fund is leveraged 200%

Life Cycle Funds

Life-cycle funds are the closest thing the industry has to a maintenance-free retirement fund. Life-cycle funds also referred to as "age-based funds" or "target-date funds", are a special breed of the balanced fund.

They are a type of fund of funds structured between equity and fixed income. But the distinguishing feature of the life-cycle fund is that its overall asset allocation automatically adjusts to become more conservative as your expected retirement date approaches.

While life-cycle funds have been around for a while, they have been gaining popularity.

LIBOR
London Interbank Offered Rate.

Liquidity
1) The degree to which an asset or security can be bought or sold in the market without affecting the asset's price. Liquidity is characterised by a high level of trading activity.
2) The ability to convert an asset to cash quickly.

Investing in illiquid assets is riskier because there might not be a way for you to get your money out of the investment. Examples of assets with good liquidity include blue-chip common stock and those assets in the money market. A fund with good liquidity would be characterised by having enough units outstanding to allow large transactions without a substantial change in price.

Liquidity Risk
The risk from a lack of liquidity, i.e. an investor having difficulty getting their money out of an investment.

Listed Security
Stock or bond that has been accepted for trading by an organised and registered securities exchange. Advantages of being listed are an orderly marketplace, more liquidity, fair price determination, accurate and continuous reporting on sales and quotations, information on listed companies and strict regulations for the protection of securities holders.

Lock Up / Lock In
Time period during which an initial investment cannot be redeemed.

Long Position
Holding a positive amount of an asset (or an asset underlying a derivative instrument).

Long / Short Hedged
Also described as the Jones Model. Manager buys securities he believes will go up in price and sells short securities he believes will decline in price. The manager will be either net long or net short and may change the net position frequently.

For example, a manager may be 60% long and 100% short, giving him a market exposure of 40% net short. The basic belief behind this strategy is that it will enhance the manager's stock-picking ability and protect investors in all market conditions.

M

Macroeconomics
The field of economics that studies the behaviour of the economy as a whole. Macroeconomics looks at economy-wide phenomena such as changes in unemployment, national income, the rate of growth, and price levels.

Managed Accounts
Accounts of individual investors which are managed individually by an investment manager. The minimum size is usually in excess of £3 million.

Managed Futures

An approach to fund management that uses positions in government securities, futures contracts, options on futures contracts and foreign exchange in a portfolio. Some managers specialise in physical commodity futures, but most find they must trade a variety of financial and non-financial contracts if they have considerable assets under management.

Management Fee

The fees taken by the manager on the entire asset level of the investment. For example, if at the end of the period the investment is valued at £1 million, and the management fee is 1.2%, then the fee would be £12,000.

Margin

The amount of assets that must be deposited in a margin account in order to secure a portion of a party's obligations under a contract.

For example, to buy or sell an exchange-traded futures contract, a party must post a specified amount that is determined by the exchange, referred to as initial margin. In addition, a party will be required to post variation margin if the futures contracts change in value. Margin is also required in connection with the purchase and sale of securities where the full purchase price is not paid upfront or the securities sold are not owned by the seller.

Market Maker

An Exchange member firm that is obliged to make a continuous two-way price that is to offer to buy and sell securities in which it is registered throughout the mandatory quote period.

Market Neutral Investing

An investment strategy that aims to produce almost the same profit regardless of market circumstances, often by taking a combination of long and short positions. This approach relies on the manager's ability to make money through relative valuation analysis, rather than through market direction forecasting. The strategy attempts to eliminate market risk and be profitable in any market condition.

Market Risk

Risk from changes in market prices.

Market Timing

1) An accepted practice of allocating assets among investments by switching into investments that appear to be beginning an uptrend and switching out of investments that appear to be starting a downtrend.

2) An increasingly unacceptable/illegal practice of undertaking frequent or large transactions in mutual funds. Especially where there is a time difference between the close of the relevant markets that the fund invests in and the valuation of the fund, i.e. a Far East fund that is valued the next day in the UK.

Market Value

The value at which an asset trades or would trade in the market.

Mark to Market

When the value of securities in a portfolio are updated to reflect the changes that have occurred due to the movement of the underlying market. The security will then be valued at its current market price.

Maximum Draw Down
The largest loss suffered by a security or fund, peak to trough, over a given period, usually one month.

Merger Arbitrage
Sometimes called Risk Arbitrage, involves investment in event-driven situations such as leveraged buy-outs, mergers and hostile takeovers. Normally the stock of an acquisition target appreciates while the acquiring company's stock decreases in value.

Mezzanine Level
Stage of a company's development just prior to it going public. Venture capitalists entering at that point have a lower risk of loss than at previous stages and can look forward to early capital appreciation as a result of the market value gained by an initial public offering.

Microeconomics
The behaviour and purchasing decisions of individuals and firms.

Money Market Funds
Mutual funds that invest in short-term highly liquid money market instruments. These funds are used when preservation of capital is paramount. They may be used to "park" money between investments, especially during periods of market uncertainty.

Mortgage Backed Security
A pass-through security that aggregates a pool of mortgage-backed debt obligations. Mortgage-backed securities' principal amounts are usually government guaranteed.

Homeowners' principal and interest payments pass from the originating bank through a government agency or investment bank, to investors, net of a loan servicing fee payable to the originator.

Multi-Manager Product

An investment pool that allocates assets to a number of managers with different investment styles. This methodology facilitates a high degree of diversification and accordingly the potential for a greater spread of risk. Hedge funds often have this structure. Smaller investors are able to enjoy access to a greater variety of managers that would normally be prohibited by minimum investment requirements for each manager. Funds of funds are a classic multi-manager product.

Municipal Bond (USA)

A debt security issued by a state, municipality, or county, in order to finance its capital expenditures. Municipal bonds are exempt from federal taxes and from most state and local taxes, especially if you live in the state the bond is issued. Such expenditures might include the construction of highways, bridges or schools. "Munis" are bought for their favourable tax implications and are popular with people in high-income tax brackets.

Mutual Fund

A security that gives small investors access to a well-diversified portfolio of equities, bonds, and other securities. Each shareholder participates in the gain or loss of the fund. Shares are issued and can be redeemed as needed. The fund's net asset value (NAV) is determined each day. Each mutual fund portfolio is invested to match the objective stated in the prospectus.

Some examples of mutual funds are UK Unit Trusts, Open-ended Investment Companies (OEICs), EU registered UCITS, Luxembourg based SICAVs.

N

NAREIT
National Association of Real Estate Investment Trusts

Nasdaq
A computerised system established by the NASD to facilitate trading by providing broker/dealers with current bid and ask price quotes on over-the-counter stocks and some listed stocks. Unlike the Amex and the NYSE, the Nasdaq (once an acronym for the National Association of Securities Dealers Automated Quotation system) does not have a physical trading floor that brings together buyers and sellers. Instead, all trading on the Nasdaq exchange is done over a network of computers and telephones. Also, the Nasdaq does not employ market specialists to buy unfilled orders as the NYSE does. The Nasdaq began when brokers started informally trading via telephone; the network was later formalised and linked by computer in the early 1970s. In 1998 the parent company of the Nasdaq purchased the Amex, although the two continue to operate separately. Orders for stock are sent out electronically on the Nasdaq, where market makers list their buy and sell prices. Once a price is agreed upon, the transaction is executed electronically.

Net Asset Value (NAV)
NAV equals the closing market value of all assets within a portfolio after subtracting all liabilities including accrued fees and expenses. NAV per share is the NAV

divided by the number of shares in issue. This is often used as the price of a fund. A purchase fee may be added to the NAV when buying units in the fund. This fee is typically 1-7%.

Net Exposure
The exposure level of a fund to the market. It is calculated by subtracting the short percentage from the long percentage. For example, if a fund is 100% long and 30% short, then the net exposure is 70% long.

Nominee Name
Name in which a security is registered and held in trust on behalf of the beneficial owner.

O

Offer Price
The price at which a fund manager or market maker will sell shares to you. (i.e. offer them to you). The offer price is higher than the Bid Price which is the price at which they will buy shares from you. (i.e. they will make a bid). This is one way in which a market maker turns a profit. A fund manager may use the difference to cover dealing administration costs.

Offshore
Located or based outside of one's national boundaries. Typically these locations have preferential tax treatments and fund legislation.

Open Architecture
In relation to funds, for example, FPIL Reserve policyholders may choose any security – open architecture. In contrast to FPIL Premier policyholders

who may only go into the FPIL mirror fund range – this is guided architecture.

Open-ended Funds
These are funds where units or shares can be bought and sold daily and where the number of units or shares in issue can vary daily.

Opportunistic Investing
A general term describing any fund that is opportunistic in nature. These types of funds are usually aggressive and seek to make money in the most efficient way at any given time. Investment themes are dominated by events that are seen as special situations or short-term opportunities to capitalise from price fluctuations or imbalances, such as initial public offering.

Option
A privilege sold by one party to another that offers the buyer the right, but not the obligation, to buy (call)or sell (put) a security at an agreed-upon price during a certain period of time or on a specific date. Options are extremely versatile securities that can be used in many different ways. Traders use options to speculate, which is a relatively risky practice, while hedgers use options to reduce the risk of holding an asset.

Over-the-Counter (OTC)
A security traded in some context other than on a formal exchange such as the LSE, NYSE, DJIA, TSX, AMEX, etc. A stock is traded over the counter usually because the company is small and unable to meet listing requirements of the exchanges. Also known as unlisted stock, these securities are traded by brokers/dealers who negotiate directly with one another over computer networks and by phone.

The Nasdaq, however, is also considered to be an OTC market, with the tier 1 being represented by companies such as Microsoft, Dell and Intel. Instruments such as bonds do not trade on a formal exchange and are thus considered over-the-counter securities. Most debt instruments are traded by investment banks making markets for specific issues.

If someone wants to buy or sell a bond, they call the bank that makes the market in that bond and asks for quotes. Many derivative instruments such as forwards, swaps and most exotic derivatives are also traded OTC.

Out of the Money
This refers to options:
1) For a call, when an option's strike price is higher than the market price of the underlying stock.
2) For a put, when the strike price is below the market price of the underlying stock.
Basically, an option that would be worthless if it expired today.

Over-Hedging
Locking in a price, such as through a futures contract, for more goods, commodities or securities that are required to protect a position. While hedging does protect a position, over-hedging can be costly in the form of missed opportunities. Although you can lock in a selling price, over-hedging might result in a producer or seller missing out on favourable market prices. For example, if you entered into a January futures contract to sell 25,000 shares of 'Smith Holdings' at $6.50 per

share you would not be able to take advantage if the spot price jumped to $7.00.

Overlay Strategy
A type of derivatives strategy. This strategy is often employed to provide protection from currencies or interest rate movements that are not the primary focus of the main portfolio strategy.

Overweight
Refers to an investment position that is larger than the generally accepted benchmark. For example, if a company normally holds a portfolio whose weighting of cash is 10%, and then increases cash holdings to 15%, the portfolio would have an overweight position in cash.

P

Pair Trading
The strategy of matching a long position with a short position in two stocks of the same sector. This creates a hedge against the sector and the overall market that the two stocks are in. The hedge created is essentially a bet that you are placing on the two stocks; the stock you are long in versus the stock you are short in. It's the ultimate strategy for stock pickers because stock picking is all that counts. What the actual market does won't matter (much). If the market or the sector moves in one direction or the other, the gain on the long stock is offset by a loss on the short.

Percent Long
The percentage of a fund invested in long positions.

Percent Short
The percentage of a fund that is sold short.

Performance Fee
The fee payable to the fund adviser on new profits earned by the fund for the period.

Portfolio Turnover
The number of times an average portfolio security is replaced during an accounting period, usually a year.

Premium
The total cost of an option. The premium of an option is basically the sum of the option's intrinsic and time value. It is important to note that volatility also affects the premium.

The difference between the higher price paid for a fixed-income security and the security's face amount at issue. If a fixed-income security (bond) is purchased at a premium, existing interest rates are lower than the coupon rate. Investors pay a premium for an investment that will return an amount greater than existing interest rates.

Price Earnings Ratio (P/E Ratio)
A valuation ratio of a company's current share price compared to its per-share earnings. Calculated as: Market Value per Share/Earnings per Share (EPS).

EPS is usually from the last four quarters (trailing P/E), but sometimes can be taken from the estimates of earnings expected in the next four quarters (projected or forward P/E). A third variation is the sum of the last two actual quarters and the estimates of the next two quarters.

Sometimes the P/E is referred to as the "multiple" because it shows how much investors are willing to pay per dollar of earnings. In general, a high P/E means high projected earnings in the future. However, the P/E ratio actually doesn't tell us a whole lot by itself. It's usually only useful to compare the P/E ratios of companies in the same industry, or to the market in general, or against the company's own historical P/E.

Prime Broker
A broker who acts as settlement agent provides custody for assets, provides financing for leverage, and prepares daily account statements for its clients, who might be money managers, hedge funds, market makers, arbitrageurs, specialists and other professional investors.

Private Placement / Private Equity
When equity capital is made available to companies or investors, but not quoted on a stock market. The funds raised through private equity can be used to develop new products and technologies, to expand working capital, to make acquisitions, or to strengthen a company's balance sheet. The average individual investor will not have access to private equity because it requires a very large investment. The result is the sale of securities to a relatively small number of investors. Private placements do not have to be registered with organisations such as the FSA, SEC because   no public offering is involved.

Proprietary Trading
When a firm trade for direct gain instead of commission dollars. Essentially, the firm has decided to profit from the market rather than commissions from processing

trades. Firms who engage in proprietary trading believe they have a competitive advantage that will enable them to earn excess returns.

Prospectus
In the case of mutual funds, a prospectus describes the fund's objectives, history, manager background, and financial statements. A prospectus makes investors aware of the risks of an investment and in most jurisdictions, is required to be published by law.

Protected Cell Company
A standard limited company that has been separated into legally distinct portions or cells. The revenue streams, assets and liabilities of each cell are kept separate from all other cells. Each cell has its own separate portion of the PCC's overall share capital, allowing shareholders to maintain sole ownership of an entire cell while owning only a small proportion of the PCC as a whole. PCCs can provide a means of entry into a captive insurance market to entities for which it was previously uneconomic. The overheads of a protected cell captive can be shared between the owners of each of the cells, making the captive cheaper to run from the point of view of the insured.

Purification
The process whereby Muslims give to charity any interest deemed to have been credited to their holdings in funds or stocks.

Put Option
An option giving the holder the right, but not the obligation, to sell a specific quantity of an asset for a fixed price during a specific period.

Q

Qualitative Analysis
Analysis that uses subjective judgment in evaluating securities based on non-financial information such as management expertise, cyclicality of industry, strength of research and development, and labour relations.

Quantitative Analysis
A security analysis that uses financial information derived from company annual reports and income statements to evaluate an investment decision. Some examples are financial ratios, the cost of capital, asset valuation, and sales and earnings trends.

Quasi-Sovereign Bond
Debt issued by a public-sector entity that is, like a sovereign bond, guaranteed by the sovereign, however, there is a difference in that there may be a timing difference in repayment in the unlikely event of default.

R

Real Estate Investment Trust (REIT)
A security that trades like a stock on the major exchanges and invests in real estate directly, through either properties or mortgages.

REITs receive special tax considerations and typically offer investors high yields, as well as a highly liquid method of investing in real estate. Equity REITs invest in and own properties (thus responsible for the equity or value of their real estate assets).

Their revenues come principally from their properties' rents. Mortgage REITs deal in investment and ownership of property mortgages. These REITs loan money for mortgages to owners of real estate or purchase existing mortgages or mortgage-backed securities. Their revenues are generated primarily by the interest that they earn on the mortgage loans. Hybrid REITs combine the investment strategies of equity REITs and mortgage REITs by investing in both properties and mortgages.

R – Squared

A statistical measure that represents the percentage of a fund's or security's movements that are explained by movements in a benchmark index. It is a measure of correlation with the benchmark. R-squared values range from 0 to 100. An R-squared of 100 means that all movements of a security are completely explained by movements in the index, i.e. perfect correlation.

Repurchase Agreement (Repo)

A form of short-term borrowing for dealers in government securities. The dealer sells the government securities to investors, usually on an overnight basis, and buys them back the following day. For the party selling the security (and agreeing to repurchase it in the future) it is a repo; for the party on the other end of the transaction (buying the security and agreeing to sell in the future) it is a reverse repurchase agreement. Repos are classified as a money-market instrument. They are usually used to raise short-term capital.

Risk-Adjusted Rate of Return

A measure of how much risk a fund or portfolio took on to earn its returns, usually expressed as a number or a rating. This is often represented by the Sharpe Ratio. The more return per unit of risk, the better.

Risk Arbitrage

A broad definition of three types of arbitrage that contain an element of risk:

1) Merger and Acquisition Arbitrage - The simultaneous purchase of stock in a company being acquired and the sale (or short sale) of stock in the acquiring company.

2) Liquidation Arbitrage - The exploitation of a difference between a company's current value and its estimated liquidation value.

3) Pairs Trading - The exploitation of a difference between two very similar companies in the same industry that have historically been highly correlated. When the two company's values diverge to a historically high level, you can take an offsetting position in each (e.g. go long in one and short the other) because, as history has shown, they will inevitably come to be similarly valued.

In theory true arbitrage is riskless; however, the world in which we operate offers very few of these opportunities. Despite these forms of arbitrage being somewhat risky, they are still relatively low-risk trading strategies which money managers (mainly hedge fund managers) and retail investors alike can employ.

Risk-Free Rate

The quoted rate on an asset that has virtually no risk. The rate quoted for US treasury bills are widely used as the risk-free rate.

Risk/Reward Ratio
This is closely related to the Sharpe Ratio, except the risk/reward ratio does not use a risk-free rate in its calculation. The higher the risk/reward ratio, the better. Calculated as: Annualised rate of return/Annualised Standard Deviation.

S

Santa Claus Rally
The rise in US stock prices that sometimes occurs in the week after Christmas, often in anticipation of the January effect.

Satellite Fund
Specialist mandate fund that offers a greater breadth of a proposition than a "core" fund.

Secondary Market
A market in which an investor purchases an asset from another investor, rather than an issuing corporation. A good example is the London Stock Exchange. All stock exchanges are part of the secondary market, as investors buy securities from other investors instead of an issuing company.

Sector Fund
A mutual fund whose objective is to invest in a particular industry or sector of the economy to capitalise on returns. Because most of the stocks in this type of fund are all in the same industry, there is a lack of diversification. The fund tends to do very well or not well at all, depending on the conditions of the specific sector.

Securities
The general name for all stocks and shares of all types.

Securities Lending
When a brokerage lends securities owned by its clients to short sellers. This allows brokers to create additional revenue (commissions) on the short sale transaction.

Semi-gilt
A financial instrument through which a municipality or parastatal (owned or controlled wholly or partly by the government) borrows money from the public in exchange for a fixed repayment plan.

SICAV
SICAV stands for Societe D'Investissement a Capital Variable. It is a Luxembourg incorporated company that is responsible for the management of a mutual fund and manages a portfolio of securities. The share capital is equal to the net assets of the fund. The units in the portfolio are delivered as shares, and the investors are referred to as shareholders. SICAVs are common fund structures in Luxembourg.

Sharia(h)
Sharia refers to the body of Islamic law. The term means "way" or "path"; it is the legal framework within which public and some private aspects of life are regulated for those living in a legal system based on Muslim principles.

Sharpe Ratio
A ratio developed by Bill Sharpe to measure risk-adjusted performance. It is calculated by subtracting the risk-free rate from the rate of return for a portfolio

and dividing the result by the standard deviation of the portfolio returns.

Calculated as: Expected Portfolio Return − Risk-Free Rate/Portfolio Standard Deviation

The Sharpe ratio tells us whether the returns of a portfolio are because of smart investment decisions or a result of excess risk. The Sortino Ratio is a variation of this.

Short Selling
The selling of a security that the seller does not own, or any sale that is completed by the delivery of a security borrowed by the seller. Short sellers assume that they will be able to buy the stock at a lower amount than the price at which they sold short. Selling short is the opposite of going long. That is, short sellers, make money if the stock goes down in price. This is an advanced trading strategy with many unique risks and pitfalls.

Small Caps
Stocks or funds with smaller capitalisation. They tend to be less liquid than blue chips, but they tend to have higher returns.

Soft Commissions
A means of paying brokerage firms for their services through commission revenue, as opposed to normal payments. For example, a mutual fund may offer to pay for the research of a brokerage firm by executing trades at the brokerage.

Sovereign Debt
A debt instrument guaranteed by a government.

Special Situations Investing

A strategy that seeks to profit from pricing discrepancies resulting from corporate event transactions such as mergers and acquisitions, spin-offs, bankruptcies or recapitalisations. Type of event-driven strategy.

Specific Risk

The risk that affects a very small number of assets. This is sometimes referred to as "unsystematic risk." An example would be news that is specific to either one stock or a small number of stocks, such as a sudden strike by the employees of a company you have shares in or a new governmental regulation affecting a particular group of companies. Unlike systematic risk or market risk, specific risk can be diversified away.

Spin-Off

A new, independent company created through selling or distributing new shares for an existing part of another company. Spinoffs may be done through a rights offering.

Sponsors

Lead investors in a fund who supply the seed money. Often the general partner in a hedge fund.

Spread

1) The difference between the bid and the offer prices of a security or asset.
2) An options position established by purchasing one option and selling another option of the same class, but of a different series.

Standard Deviation
Tells us how much the return on the fund is deviating from the expected normal returns.

Stop-Loss Order
An order placed with a broker to sell a security when it reaches a certain price. It is designed to limit an investor's loss on a security position. This is sometimes called a "stop market order." In other words, setting a stop-loss order for 10% below the price you paid for the stock would limit your loss to 10%.

Strategic Bond Funds
Invest primarily in higher-yielding assets including high yield bonds, investment grade bonds, preference shares and other bonds. The funds take strategic asset allocation decisions between countries, asset classes, sectors and credit ratings.

Strike Price
The stated price per share for which underlying stock may be purchased (for a call) or sold (for a put) by the option holder upon exercise of the option contract.

Swap
Traditionally, the exchange of one security for another to change the maturity (bonds), quality of issues (stocks or bonds), or because investment objectives have changed. Recently, swaps have grown to include currency swaps and interest rates swaps.

If firms in separate countries have comparative advantages on interest rates, then a swap could benefit both firms. For example, one firm may have a lower fixed interest rate, while another has access to a lower floating interest rate. These firms could swap to take advantage of the lower rates.

Swaption (Swap Option)
The option to enter into an interest rate swap. In exchange for an option premium, the buyer gains the right but not the obligation to enter into a specified swap agreement with the issuer on a specified future date.

Swing Trading (Swings)
A style of trading that attempts to capture gains in a stock within one to four days. To find situations in which a stock has this extraordinary potential to move in such a short time frame, the trader must act quickly. This is mainly used by at-home and day traders. Large institutions trade in sizes too big to move in and out of stocks quickly. The individual trader is able to exploit the short-term stock movements without the competition of major traders. Swing traders use technical analysis to look for stocks with short-term price momentum. These traders aren't interested in the fundamental or intrinsic value of stocks but rather in their price trends and patterns.

Systematic Risk
The risk inherent to the entire market or entire market segment. Also known as "un-diversifiable risk" or "market risk" interest rates, recession and wars all represent sources of systematic risk because they will affect the entire market and cannot be avoided through diversification. Whereas this type of risk affects a broad range of securities, unsystematic risk affects a very specific group of securities or an individual security. Systematic risk can be mitigated only by being hedged.

Systemic Risk

The risk that threatens an entire financial system.

S&P500

Standard & Poor's Index of the New York Stock Exchange. A basket of 500 stocks that are considered to be widely held. The S&P 500 index is weighted by market value, and its performance is thought to be representative of the stock market as a whole.

T

Treasury Bill

A negotiable debt obligation issued by the U.S. government and backed by its full faith and credit, having a maturity of one year or less. Exempt from state and local taxes. Also called Bill or T-Bill or U.S. Treasury Bill.

Time Value

The amount by which an option's premium exceeds its intrinsic value. Also called time premium.

Top-Down Investing

An investment strategy which first finds the best sectors or industries to invest in, and then searches for the best companies within those sectors or industries. This investing strategy begins with a look at the overall economic picture and then narrows it down to sectors, industries and companies that are expected to perform well. Analysis of the fundamentals of a given security is the final step.

Tracking Error

This statistic measures the standard deviation of a fund's excess returns over the returns of an index or benchmark portfolio. As such, it can be an indication of 'riskiness' in the manager's investment style. A Tracking Error below 2 suggests a passive approach, with a close fit between the fund and its benchmark. At 3 and above the correlation is progressively looser: the manager will be deploying a more active investment style and taking bigger positions away from the benchmark's composition.

Traded Endowment Policy (TEP)
An Endowment Policy is a type of life insurance that has a value that is payable to the insured if he/she is still living on the policy's maturity date, or to a beneficiary otherwise. They are normally "with profits policies". If the insured does not wish to wait until maturity to receive the value, they can either surrender it back to the issuing insurance company, or they can sell the policy on the open market. If the policy is sold it then becomes a Traded Endowment Policy or TEP. TEP Funds aim to buy and sell TEPs at advantageous prices to make a profit.

Traded Options
Transferable options with the right to buy or sell a standardised amount of a security at a fixed price within a specified period.

Traditional Investments
Includes equities, bonds, high yield bonds, emerging markets debt, cash, cash equivalents.

U

Umbrella Fund
An investment company which has a group of sub-funds (pools) each having its own investment portfolio.

The purpose of this structure is to provide investment flexibility and widen investor choice.

Underlier or Underlying Security
A security or commodity, which is subject to delivery upon exercise of an option contract or convertible security. Exceptions include index options and futures, which cannot be delivered and are therefore settled in cash.

Underweight
A situation where a portfolio does not hold a sufficient amount of securities to satisfy the accepted benchmark of the portfolio's asset allocation strategy. For example, if a portfolio normally holds 40% stock and currently holds 30%, the position in equities would be considered underweight.

Unit Trust
A common form of collective investment (similar to a mutual fund) where investors' money is pooled and invested into a variety of shares and bonds in order to reduce risk. Its capital structure is open-ended as units can be created or redeemed depending on demand from investors. It should be noted that a Unit Trust means something completely different in the US.

V

Value of New Business (VNB)
Sum of all income i.e. charges, from new policies minus costs of setting up the policies i.e. commission, discounted to present day value.

Value Stocks
Stocks which are perceived to be selling at a discount to their intrinsic or potential worth, i.e. undervalued; or stocks which are out of favour with the market and are under-followed by analysts. It is believed that the share price of these stocks will increase as the value of the company is recognised by the market.

Value-Added Monthly Index (VAMI)
An index that tracks the monthly performance of a hypothetical $1000 investment. The calculation for the current month's VAMI is: Previous VAMI x (1 + Current Rate of Return).

The value-added monthly index charts the total return gained by an investor from reinvestment of any dividends and additional interest gained through compounding. The VAMI index is sometimes used to evaluate the performance of a fund manager.

Venture Capital
Money and resources made available to start-up firms and small businesses with exceptional growth potential. Venture capital often also includes managerial and technical expertise. Most venture capital money comes from an organised group of wealthy investors who seek substantially above average returns and who are willing to accept correspondingly high risks. This form of raising capital is increasingly popular among new companies that, because of a limited operating history, can't raise money through a debt issue. The downside for entrepreneurs is that venture capitalists usually receive a say in the major decisions of the company in addition to a portion of the equity.

Volatility

Standard deviation is a statistical measurement which, when applied to an investment fund, expresses its volatility, or risk. It shows how widely a range of returns varied from the fund's average return over a particular period. Low volatility reduces the risk of buying into an investment in the upper range of its deviation cycle, then seeing its value head towards the lower extreme. For example, if a fund had an average return of 5%, and its volatility was 15, this would mean that the range of its returns over the period had swung between +20% and -10%. Another fund with the same average return and 5% volatility would return between 10% and nothing, but there would at least be no loss.

Printed in Great Britain
by Amazon